D1215050

HORSE TRAILS

Along

The Desert

The author on the western desert early in the century.

HORSE TRAILS

Along

The Desert

SANFORD C. YODER

Illustrated by

EZRA HERSHBERGER

HERALD PRESS
SCOTTDALE, PENNSYLVANIA

Copyright 1954 by Herald Press, Scottdale, Pennsylvania

Library of Congress Catalogue Card Number: 54-11446

Other books by the author

For Conscience Sake

Poetry of the Old Testament

Down South America Way

Eastward to the Sun

[PRINTED
IN U·S·A]

To

My children Myron Stutsman, Anna Marguerite

Etta LaVerne and their children

CONTENTS

All the past we leave behind,
We debouch upon a newer, mightier world,
  varied world,
Fresh and strong the world we seize, world
  of labor and of march,
  Pioneers! O pioneers!

Walt Whitman

I

The Call of the West

Abraham Lincoln's father is credited with having said that when your neighbors get close enough that you can see the smoke from their chimneys, the country is becoming too thickly settled. Something of this spirit must have possessed my ancestors at the time when some of them ventured to leave their quiet European homes for the vast wilderness that has now become the United States. Here they became a part of that illustrious company of pioneers that felled the forests, drained the marshes and swamplands, built cities and villages, and turned the empty spaces into prosperous settlements and happy communities that by now fill the land from sea to sea. After having lived in Pennsylvania and Ohio they migrated to Iowa which was then a new and thinly populated country. Still later, within my recollection, when the smoking chimneys of their neighbors surrounded them, my parents, together with some of their in-laws and

1

other relatives, found a home on the level prairie lands of northern Iowa where the population was more sparse and the wide open spaces afforded them the ample room they desired.

Sometime during the last half of the nineteenth century a few families from my father's side of the house moved to Wyoming and located on the open range far to the north and east of Cheyenne, which was then an untamed frontier town. Here they went into the stock business. Now and then they would bring back carloads of horses which were sold to the horse-buying population, either privately or at public auction.

I recall the tall figure of Phil Yoder swaggering along in the gait of one that is used to the saddle. His high-heeled boots and what is now known as a ten-gallon hat, tight-fitting trousers and a highly colored silk muffler made him a striking and picturesque figure which stirred the blood of the youngsters who saw him. At that time the war between the sheepmen and the cattlemen was hot, and his tales of their struggle, together with stories and descriptions of the roundup, the long freighting trips to Cheyenne when he camped at night beside his wagon and sometimes slept in the snow, made a deep impression on us boys. It served to stimulate the spirit of adventure within me from which I never fully recovered, not even after the hard years we spent in the Great American Desert.

I presume that all boys at some time become possessed with a desire to get away from the routine of the settled life to which they are more or less bound during the years while they are growing up and they long to rove and roam without much aim or purpose in an atmosphere which is less restrained. This innate restlessness within me was early stirred into activity by incidents such as I have already described.

However, as the years went by, other interests arose. The

2

hard work and long hours on an Iowa farm did not offer much inspiration to me. Attendance at high school was an adventure. New learning, in fields of knowledge unknown to me, opened wide vistas that begged for exploration. The ambition to enter a profession and finally the necessity of providing for a home and family became steadying influences in my life as they are in the lives of others when maturity takes the place of adolescent dreams and desires.

When, however, prospects of entering the profession upon which my heart was set, faded, my mind again turned to the West which was said to be full of opportunity for the young and strong and daring. Accordingly, we—my wife, our little son, and I—decided to migrate to the state of Washington. Here I taught school one year or nearly so, until illness made it necessary for me to give up my position. Then we turned to the great open spaces that lay between the Rockies and the Cascades where I entered claim to a homestead consisting of one hundred and sixty acres. My wife's brother had taken up land in the area and in addition to that we had each purchased another quarter and had acquired control over other lands. Besides this we had access to the miles and miles of open range that lay around us between the Columbia River, the Saddle Mountains, and the Koontz Coulee.

Youth is gullible. Lack of experience and untried dreams drew us into a situation that neither of us foresaw. It was filled with the freedom of the wide spaces, away from smoking chimneys and crowded communities where one can easily intrude on someone else's rights. Here in these isolated places there was liberty, but a person had to become master of the circumstances that he constantly faced or his surroundings would master him and draw him mercilessly to his end. If a person doesn't grow up and mature under conditions such as these, there is little hope that he ever will.

There were long dusty miles between us and the railroad, our base of supplies, and most of the settlers had to haul their water from the river. All provisions had to be purchased and hauled in. To overcome the obstacles one meets in such a place is a man's task. This venture presented a challenge that we accepted, and while we would not say that we mastered our situation, yet we did not leave the place because we had to.

We built our cabin—rather I did—on a little knoll in the midst of our holdings on what was known as Sunflower Flat. Like Jacob of old, when he returned from his sojourn at Haran, we built shelters for our stock and constructed a rude corral. To the north of us lay the bleak Saddle Mountains several thousand feet above the surrounding country. West of us was the Columbia River, a mile or more wide in places, which could be crossed only by a ferry or rowboat. Beyond that to the place where the sun so often splashed its colors across the evening sky lay the Cascade Mountains with the snowy head of Mt. Ranier rising above them all. During the hot summer months when the shadows of evening fell, it sent its coolness across the barren wastes and gave us pleasant nights. To the southwest lay the Rattlesnake Mountains and to the south and east there were long stretches of sagebrush-covered desert that reached onward till they were lost in the horizon.

Occasionally, when atmospheric conditions were right, the Blue Mountains, miles to the east, were seen in the sky. Such mirages were not infrequent. Sometimes on hot summer days the most enchanting and enticing bodies of water appeared at places where we knew there were none. But they looked so real that only those experienced in the ways of the desert were able to resist their allurement. Years earlier when unseasoned immigrants made their way westward many of them were lured to their death by these delusions which nature throws upon her screen.

The country was covered with a growth of sagebrush, a typical desert plant which sometimes reaches a height of six

4

or more feet. Aside from that there was a scant growth of small grass known as sheep grass, and a scattered growth of sunflowers and other plants which furnished pasture for the life which existed here. Coyotes, the evening wolves of the Scripture, were plentiful and filled the twilight air as well as the night with doleful howls which to the newcomer are at first frightening but which later become the evening songs that lull the veteran of the range to sleep.

The land to which we came was a horse and sheep country. There were a few cattle along the river but the grasses were scant, which meant that stock had to go a long distance from its watering place in order to get enough feed to live. Even in the hottest weather these range horses (cayuses) got water but once in five to seven or eight days. They usually lay around the streams or springs and ponds a whole day and left in the evening, grazing as they traveled leisurely along. Sheep were on the range only in wintertime and then they somehow managed to get along with little water.

At the time of our sojourn the land was being sold to people from the East for wheat growing and dry farming. Every alternate section was owned by the government. Those bearing the even numbers could be homesteaded. That is, a person could secure title to a quarter section (160 acres) by filing his claim at the local Federal Land Office. After that he had eight months within which to establish residence on it and live there at least six months each year for five consecutive years. During that period he was required to make sufficient improvements on the place to assure the government that he was acting in good faith. At the end of that time he was eligible to receive title to the land. Or, if desirable, he could live on the claim six months after which he could commute and receive title by paying the sum of four hundred dollars. Such a deed now rests among my legal papers as a memorial of the time we spent in the desert. It bears the signature of William Howard Taft, who then occupied the presidential chair at Washington, D.C. The rest of the land—all the odd-numbered sections—belonged to the railroads, which they received as an inducement to extend their lines across the wide unsettled spaces to the western sea. When it was later sold to large real estate agencies or stockmen and settlers it brought in a substantial sum of money to the railroad companies.

In such an environment our home was located during our four years' residence in the desert. At that time horses had a value, and buying, selling, and trading furnished in part the means of our livelihood. Other sources of our subsistence came from clearing land for homesteaders and freighting supplies from the railroad some twenty miles away.

The winters were delightful—most of the time. Occasionally there was a little snow and a few times the temperature went down to zero and below—one time it fell to twenty-five degrees below! Most of the five to seven inches of rain that fell within the year came from October to May. In the spring lovely little flowers popped out of earth and shed their fragrance on the desert air. There was no one to enjoy the sweetness of these little blooms! Then one day the first breath of heated wind came from the Northeast, across the fields of hot sand and rock and barrenness. After that it came regularly with increasing intensity beginning about ten o'clock in the forenoon and continuing until evening. Then it went down with the setting sun and the cool breezes of the hills blew in upon us and gave us restful and pleasant nights. One day, when we looked for the flowers we had so admired, we found that they had disappeared under our eyes. The vegetation—such as there was—had become brown dry and the sagebrush with an innate wisdom bestowed upon it by the Giver of life curled up its leaves tightly to keep what moisture it had stored up within its being from escaping into the thirsty atmosphere. The sky

6

turned to an ashen gray with seldom a cloud except over the top of the Cascades, where they dropped their moisture on the high ranges and then disappeared.

People were few in number. There were times when our closest neighbors lived six miles away. During the spring roundup horsemen appeared now and then; but since the corrals were located along the river at Muir's Landing, Nagle's, White Bluff, and Waluke, these men seldom stopped. Perhaps our most frequent visitor was Buckaroo Brown who apparently was a scout for one of the horse companies. He came to our place often and furnished us companionable hours which we greatly appreciated.

Churches, such as there were, were twenty miles away; consequently attendance was out of the question. Since we were the only outfit that was equipped with wagons, work stock, and saddle horses, we got to the railroad more frequently than did the other settlers. When we went, we brought the mail and supplies for the community. Sunday was the time when they came to our place to get their letters and papers and to exchange such news as there was. Among them was Abe Harder, a linotype operator and a lawyer but mostly a hobo. He took up a claim with the intention of raising chickens, but when everything had happened that usually comes to pass when a lawyer bestows his practice upon poultry, an occupation that is far removed from his profession, he had only one fowl left—a Blue Andalusian rooster which he named Andy. Abe was a regular visitor at our place. The last time he came he was leading—or carrying—Andy across the weary distance that lay between our place and his. Upon leaving he turned him over to us whereupon he soon found his way into the frying pan. A missionary and his wife, Reverend and Mrs. George Guthrie, who had spent a term of service in India, had taken up a claim adjoining ours. During their eight months' residence we spent many happy Sundays together. Several times we

7

had church services at our cabin for such as cared to come.

As this mixed group of settlers now passes before me I find it an interesting collection of folks. Most of them came from the cities, and many of them were women. There were schoolteachers, some of whom held responsible positions in the best schools of the large centers. There were four girls whose father was a lawyer in Spokane. Another was an oculist from Kansas City. Several elderly widows or maiden ladies brought their elegant wardrobes and jewels with them when they came, only to find themselves pretty much in the position of the dead Irishman "who was all dressed up and had no place to go."

Life in those parts was hard. Our saddle horses were kept in the pasture which furnished them the feed they needed, but the work stock had to be fed. All of the provisions for horses as well as for the family had to be freighted in from the railroad. Gardens were out of the question on account of the sparse rainfall. The only food which the country furnished was jack rabbit meat of which there was an abundance. Either the rifle or shotgun was on the seat of our heavy freighting wagon all the time and now and then we succeeded in getting a sage hen for the larder and more rarely a duck or goose when they migrated across the country.

After the first year or so most of the homesteaders disappeared. No one felt too badly about it because too many people spoil a country where stock depends upon the open range for its life. After this exodus the land was full of empty cabins. Most of them were less than that; they were mere shacks that were occupied by such residents as were native to the country. Skunks, badgers, trade rats, if there was something to trade, took possession in the absence of the owners.

One morning I rode across the mile-and-a-half-wide pasture to bring in some stock when I noticed smoke rising from one of the vacated cabins on the section adjoining ours. Immediately my curiosity was stirred. The forms of a few unfamiliar men straggled around in the sagebrush; they were strangers in the land. Frequently undesirable men, some of whom may have been in conflict with the law, hibernated in such out-of-the-way places to escape the vigilance of the officers. At such times people were alerted about any suspicious characters that might show up. Then the United States Marshal and sundry and divers other officers would go into action. Thinking that these newcomers might be hiding out, I decided to ride up and find out who they were. Instead of being outlaws as I presumed they might be they introduced themselves by such familiar names as Bair and Summers from the Canton-Louisville, Ohio, community. They had come West to make their fortunes, and land agents at Spokane had directed them to this area where they said homesteads were still available and incidentally charged them a fee to locate claims for them. They remained in the country during our residence there. Part of the time they worked for me and all the while they formed a circle of friends that helped make the lonely days in the Great American Desert bearable.

The years, though filled with hardship, exposure, and all the rigors that go with the life one lives in such places, passed quickly and we were drawn deeply into our surroundings—more deeply than we knew—so that when the time came to leave the place, we realized how strangely and strongly we had become attached to our home on the range. The drifting herds of range horses, the coyotes, the meadow larks, the smoke-dimmed mountains, and even the sagebrush had become our friends whom we were reluctant to desert.

I know of a land where the rolling plains
　　Stretch out in the vast expanse;
Where the Northeast winds forever blow,
　　And the shimmering heat waves dance;
Where the cattle graze on a thousand hills,
　　And the untamed cayuses roam;
And the coyote howls at the silver moon,
　　In sight of the rancher's home.

I know of a land where the cowboy rides
　　In a reckless, headlong pace,
And clings to the back of his outlaw steed
　　With a careless, easy grace;
Where the quick eye gleams like a lightning flash,
　　If danger ventures near;
And the whirring rope flies true
　　And snares the fleeing steer.

I know of a land where the hearts are true,
　　And the minds of men are free;
Where a man is known for what he is,
　　And not for what he used to be.
If a man's a man he can lift his head
　　And stand among the best.
So I long to go to a place I know
　　In the land of the Golden West.

Author Unknown

II

Getting the Feel of the Country

When I arrived at Prosser, Washington, it was spring-time. The town at that time had a population of around two thousand inhabitants. It is situated on the south bank of the Yakima River under the shadow of Horseheaven whose north wall rises abruptly hundreds of feet like a mountain and from its crest crowned with a range of low peaks, it slopes gradually southward toward the Columbia River some eighty miles away. At the time of my arrival the town was a mixture of the old and the new West. Several miles to the north of the river the land was under irrigation. Orchards were in bloom and lush alfalfa fields were green with the growth of springtime. On the higher slopes of the Rattlesnake Mountains miles to the north, and on top of the Horseheaven country to the south, there were scattered fields of wheat from which the dry land farmers occasionally harvested a good crop. The rest of the wide area was open range where the roving bands of wild horses eked out their existence on the sparse grasses which grew there. Where water was available there were a few herds of cattle.

The town had modern stores of various kinds such as one finds in other parts of the country. It had churches, schools, and all the other social organizations which a cultured society brings with it. But it also contained remnants of the old. There were nearly as many saloons as grocery stores—perhaps more. These places were conducted very much on the order of the earlier days. Women, however, were not permitted in the barroom, but each place had an outdoor space in the rear, enclosed with a high board fence, where this kind of patron was waited upon. Just outside of the corporation limits were the haunts of evil where gambling, drinking, and all kinds of vice and sin flourished in their worst forms.

On the streets and sidewalks moved a motley array of people: women well dressed and cultured; business and professional men moving side by side with the men from the range. Buckaroos with goatskin chaps, broad-brimmed hats, and high-heeled boots, and now and then a sheepherder with his faithful collies, were still much in evidence. At certain times of the year there was hardly a day that didn't bring in bands of the red men with their squaws and papooses and their array of children, dogs, and all else that is dear to the Indian heart. Most of them were by this time subdued and had submitted to their fate, which they accepted with resignation, but not without a lot of ill feeling. Some of the older ones who had lived and fought through Indian wars still bristled with hate and missed no opportunity of letting the white man know what they thought of him or where in their opinion he ought to be.

Early one morning a small band of Umatillas showed up on the streets and stabled their horses at the livery barn.

An old blanket Indian, whose face was scarred and hard, dismounted and went through the motions of a war dance, all the while with fiercely glowering eyes, muttering things about the white man and his final destination. The latter evidently constituted the extent of his theological knowledge—on that he was well posted!

When the time came for moving the sheep to the summer pastures, camp wagons loaded with equipment and supplies passed along the streets and sheepherders paused at the saloons and the other places in the town for the solace that vice affords before going to the great solitudes of the grazing lands high up in the mountains, far removed from the haunts of men. Stockmen became "Western" again as they assumed their roundup regalia when the time for the spring roundup came and buckaroos with the necessary trappings and equipment for the days of hard riding took one last fling at the bar and staged what to a tenderfoot looked like a wild celebration before they followed the chuck wagon to the range for their summer's work. To a seasoned old-timer, however, these performances must have looked like a mere flash in the pan when compared with the old days of Dodge City, Tombstone, Tucson, and similar places that roared in the times which they remembered.

Such was the place to which I came when I, together with two other men who accompanied me in this adventure, stepped off the Northern Pacific train that early April morning. We were hardly off the platform until a real-estate agent spotted us and followed us to a restaurant across the street from the depot. We discovered that the town simply swarmed with his ilk.

Before the day was over I fell into the hands of one of the old settlers who gave me good advice. Sometime later I purchased a lot in the new addition about a mile from the business part of town, close to the highway that followed the banks of the Yakima River. With the help of the two boys who had accompanied me I built a house which became our home during the first year of our sojourn in the West. This was my first building venture. Material was cheap and the entire cost of this four-room house was less than three hundred dollars. When it was completed my wife and little son arrived to take up residence in the state and become citizens of the sagebrush.

I was not long in the town until I witnessed an eruption of the thin veneer of the new culture that was spreading itself over the old. A few evenings before the arrival of my family I left the hotel where I was staying and joined a group of men who had collected as usual on the sidewalk benches at the corner where the two principal streets crossed. We were suddenly startled by pistol shots close by and for the first time I heard the whine of lead singing its high-keyed tone as it passed over my head. Not half a block away two gamblers had met and "shot it out" as they say. The one next to us had his arm splintered and was disabled. The other one made a dash to get out of town but was overtaken by the sheriff and brought back and was lodged in jail. I had often seen both men in town. They were well-dressed, harmless-appearing fellows and most people would not have judged from their looks that either one had lethal inclinations or ambitions. It turned out that there were gambling scores that were unsettled and besides that a woman figured in the case. I was summoned to appear in court as a witness on the afternoon of the arrival of my wife and little son. The courtroom was crowded and buzzed with excitement, but nothing happened to either of the men. The case was committed to the superior court but it never came to trial. Here I learned that in that part of the country witnesses never testified until they had received their pay, which course I had not followed. Hence, the state of Washington still owes me my witness fees, which together with accrued interest would by now add up to a substantial figure. However, the sorry facts in the case are that by this time the account has become invalidated by the statute of limitation and is not collectable.

Among the very interesting characters we learned to know was old man Kinney, who is said to have pitched his tent at this place long before there were buildings on the present townsite. He claimed the honor of having given the name "Horseheaven" to the elevation that looked like a low mountain range which stretched along the Yakima River for miles east and west. He told us that when he camped within the shadow of those hills for the first time, he hobbled the leader of his herd, as was the custom in those days, and turned the whole band loose to graze for the night. The next morning his horses had disappeared and were nowhere to be found. After a long search along the coulees, the ravines, the hills and valleys, he finally followed one of the few trails to the top and found them reveling in bunch grass to their knees. This was a horse's paradise and he called it Horseheaven, the name which it still bears.

This old pioneer lived far back in the past. He never ceased to grieve over the intrusion of settlers that spoiled the range for stockmen. He occupied his old dilapidated shack that stood within the shadow of the hills near the edge of the town, which was yearly encroaching upon him and threatened to dispossess him entirely of his heritage, his property, and his freedom. In fact, the latter had already been lost. He maintained a small band of horses who were his only friends and they were an ungracious and inconsiderate lot. When they were not in the city pound they trespassed on the property of irate neighbors who resorted to all kinds of means to rid themselves of these fragments of the days of freedom that had never become adjusted to what people think of as an orderly society. What happened to this old man—remnant of a passing age— I never learned to know. No doubt when he crossed the

Last Divide what few friends he had wrapped him in his saddle blanket with his pitifully crumpled boots for a pillow and buried him under the brow of the bluff where he made his last stand against the onward march of time. Then the eternal years closed over him.

Just below the banks of the Yakima near our home was a clear spring of fresh, cooling water, where travelers, Indians, horsemen, freighters, and others who passed that way through the country stopped to refresh themselves and their mounts and herds. This brought past our door a colorful array of people. Most interesting to us were the groups of Indians who passed by and often stopped to prepare their food and rest a while. A few miles to the west of us was the east boundary of the Yakima reservation. During the summer and fall the Umatillas and the Pendletons from the East Oregon country were much on the move to the berry and hop fields of the west coast where they were employed as pickers.

But most exciting of all were the days when the men came in from the roundup. One afternoon, miles up the valley and far up on the slopes of Horseheaven, a streak of dust hung heavily over one of the trails that came out of the hills. Those who were familiar with the ways of the country knew that the boys were bringing in a herd of horses from the roundup. Bartenders made ready to receive them. So did all the other places which were usually frequented by the men who were hungry for the excitement which the horsetown had to offer. Later in the evening the dusty herd was brought in and corraled at the east end of town.

The next day the stock was to be separated and divided to the owners according to their brands. When the work began each man was mounted on his best cutting horse, which meant the one that was best trained and the most skilled in cutting out horses from the herd and putting them into the section of the enclosure set apart for each owner. The top rail of the corral was lined with spectators consisting of a sprinkling of old buckaroos who compared the present performances of horses and men with those of their day when everything was, in their opinion, par-excellent. There were some buyers, greenhorns and "tenderfooters"—newcomers. I am not sure where I was classified—certainly in one of the last two categories. This was a show! Men mounted on horses with ropes in hand, ready for a throw, if necessary, were directing their saddle horses—or were they? Perhaps they just let them have their way, for they seemed to know as much about this business as did the occupants of the saddle —if not more. If one can read the mind of a horse, then I would say that they thoroughly enjoyed their task.

Out of the dust and confusion of the milling herd darted a beautiful chestnut sorrel mare, a three-year-old, with silver mane and tail and white stockings on her hind legs that reached to the knees and white anklets on the fore legs. She was cut out of the herd and shoved off into a side corral. This was one of the most beautifully built animals I ever saw and I decided that if she was for sale she would be mine. I immediately got down from my perch on the rail and approached the boss of the roundup about the possibility of buying her. I discovered that she bore an outlaw brand and as such she belonged to the roundup. After some consultation with others he offered to sell her for thirty-five dollars. She was as wild and untamed as the wind that blew. They promised to deliver her outside the corral at the end of the rope. From there on she was my responsibility. As I remember it now they offered to deliver her at my home for another five dollars, but I decided that I might as well begin learning this wild cayuse business at once, if I was going to learn it at all.

I went to the harness shop and purchased my first lariat. One of the men threw the rope on her and taught me how to make a hackamore. Then with the help of others we got

17

her outside the corral and she was mine! Since that time I have handled hundreds of horses but never one like this one. With the use of such horse sense as I had I managed to get her to our home on the other side of town. Each day from then on I practiced roping her and worked with her. Finally she allowed me to put the saddle on her. By rewarding her with a palmful of salt when I caught her she finally came to me of her own will when I entered the corral. Later I cautiously mounted her—I, however, did not let her know that I was cautious! Within a short time she was a saddle horse, beautifully gaited and an excellent saddler. She became the pride of our outfit and was coveted by all the stockmen who saw her. Again and again I refused offers for her that seemed unreasonable; but she was gentle, trustworthy, fleet-footed and sure. She was a mount my wife could ride and a playmate for our little son who had very few companions after we moved onto our holdings in the desert.

Within a few days the men, clad in the regalia of the range, were ready to return to the roundup. Along about noon they began to gather at the barroom next to the railroad for a last fling before they returned to the bleak hills to finish their work of the season. It was a wild time! They threw their money on the bar and everything was free for everybody—that is, it was paid for. Among them were men with such names as Highfil, Indian Charley, Californy Joe, Montana Bill, and others whose names were designed, perhaps, to obscure their identity. No one inquired too closely. It wasn't good range country ethics to do so. Californy Joe had probably never seen California and Montana Bill may never have been near Montana. When the sun was on its way downward toward the horizon they rode away into the afternoon, to follow the herds, drink their black coffee, and eat the biscuits and ˙beans and "sowbosom" by the side of the chuck wagon for another several months or so until the rodeo was over.

But there was another side to the life of this growing town. Settlers from all parts of the country were located in the irrigated section north of the river. Many of them were a high type of citizens who were in the process of turning the Old West into the New, in which the spirit of hospitality, openheartedness, and friendliness was to prevail for many more years, unfettered by the social barriers and community traditions of the older settlements.

During my year's stay at Prosser I was elected principal of the Pioneer School in which the seventh and eighth grades were taught. I appreciated this work and might have remained in the profession except that my health broke toward the close of the year, and the freedom of the wide spaces was too alluring to resist. I shall always remember the boys and girls that I worked with. There was Harold Guernsey, the undertaker's son, who undertook to write his own excuses for the numerous, unjustifiable absences which he accumulated. And there was Freddie McNeil, whose father was sheriff. There was also the seemingly incorrigible girl whose father was a milkman. She liked to draw uncomplimentary pictures of her teachers. One day I passed her desk and spied one of her masterpieces entitled "My Teacher." It certainly lacked nothing that was ugly. She had much to work on, and had overlooked no detail. If possible, she had exaggerated some. I picked it up and called the attention of the school to it and commented at some length on her ability as an artist. After that it was posted on the wall. When the member of the school board who looked after the building and the goings on within its halls heard of the episode he was so scared that he almost trembled. He informed me that her parents would cause me trouble. They always do, he said. But I never heard from them. From then on she was the most humble, docile girl in the class. Her conduct was all that could be desired. Her grades went up and when I left the school she was my friend.

19

I see those youngsters now, all of them, as they were then, happy, some petty and quarrelsome, keen-minded, full of life and the spirit of the times in which they lived. I often wonder where they are now and what time has done to them. Some years after I moved back to the East I returned to Prosser to look after some business matters. The sheriff informed me that Freddie died of an injury he had received while playing. Poor Freddie, he was such an honest boy and I looked for great things from him. One day he accompanied his friend, the excuse writer, on one of his forays into the Horseheaven gulches and presented an excuse the next morning which I knew he had written himself. When school was dismissed in the evening he lingered on. It seemed that he couldn't leave and he couldn't talk. When I had finished my work he was still standing by the window. So I called him to my desk and asked him about his trouble. After talking it over I destroyed his excuse and never had any reason to doubt his integrity thereafter.

The closing incident of our residence at Prosser was the tragic death of George Evans, one of our neighbors, the son of an old frontiersman who befriended us so often when we lived in the city and helped us get oriented to our new surroundings. George was a quiet, harmless fellow, but there was some trouble over an affair so trivial that most people would have paid no attention to it. One evening when he was leaving one of the barrooms his enemy drew on him and shot. A few days later George died. This was a passing flash out of the Old West, the spirit of which was still close to the surface. Four years later while traveling from Portland, Oregon, to Seattle, Washington, I met the nephew of the gunman who had committed the crime and was informed that the case had just come to trial and the murderer had been set free.

During the year of our residence at Prosser, I had filed on a homestead beyond the Rattlesnakes in the Columbia

20

River country, and now the time was here to move to the claim. The alfalfa fields were greening, the apple trees were in blossom, the camp wagons of the sheepmen were beginning to move as the herders trailed the flocks to the mountains. The buckaroos were gathering in for the annual roundup.

> The air was shot through with springtime
> And the breezes smelled of May.[1]

The long road to the open spaces was calling and we were on the way!

[1] Hostetler, E. LaVerne, "Springtime," in the files of the author.

I am never at rest with the desert before me,
Its sages and greasewoods are voices that call.
The sigh of its night-wind like love-whispers entreat me,
I can never be quiet when snow peaks stand high,
And entice me endlessly to push on to the sky.

Sanford C. Yoder

III

The Lure of the Open Spaces

I was not in Prosser long until I was elected principal of one of the schools and teacher of the eighth grade. I considered myself fortunate but the lure of land was in the air and I began to look around for a homestead. Most of the good tracts in the area where we lived had already been entered, though now and then a relinquishment could be bought. Finally I discovered one in what was known as the Glade Country about thirty-five miles out on the south slope of Horseheaven. Upon investigation I found it very satisfactory. Lumber for the cabin was already on the claim.

There were also sufficient posts and wire to enclose the quarter section. It lay on a prominent elevation, high above a deep coulee in the bottom of which were several springs of clear, cool water. Nearby was a sheep camp occupied only in wintertime. Horse corrals which were the center of the roundup for this area were a mile or so farther up the coulee. It was far from the railroad (thirty-five miles) and about equally distant from the Columbia River. It was nevertheless a very desirable piece of land. One corner of it dipped down over the rim of the canyon. The rest of it was level, free from scab rock, with deep soil composed of volcanic ash. To the west a few miles the undulating land-scape broke into the foothills of the Cascades which farther on were crowned with the perpetual snows of Mt. Adams.

A few days after this investigation was made I rode out to the place in order to accompany the owner to the Federal Land Office at Cleveland, deep in the foothills of the mountains, where he was to file his relinquishment and I at the same time was to enter my claim. This was a thrilling trip. During my ride across the Horseheaven country I found myself alone for the first time in the wide untamed, open spaces of the West. Bands of range horses wandered through the sagebrush. At this season of the year they were wary of anyone mounted on a saddle horse and at first sight they headed for the shelter of some coulee or butte where they felt secure. A lone sheepherder with his flock of sheep was belatedly lingering here on the plains waiting for the camp equipment to precede him to the mountains for the summer pasture.

Not long after leaving the homestead for the land office we began to pass the juniper trees or shrubs that were the outposts of the vast tall pines and firs on the far mountainsides. What a refreshing place Cleveland was after a day's ride in the desert! Roses bloomed all along the streets. The lawns were green and well kept. Clear water from the

24

springs on the hillsides flowed along the gutters and the cool, rare atmosphere of the mountain altitudes was a great relief from the dry, dust-laden heat of the lowlands.

Within a half hour the transaction was made and I had filed on one of the most desirable claims in all that country. It was nearly sundown when we left the land office, some sixty-five miles from home. I rode on until nearly midnight when I dismounted, and slept for the first time under the open sky far from any human habitation except for the scattered settlers that were few and far between. After a few hours of rest I remounted and sometime early in the morning I saw from the crest of Horseheaven the sun come up out of the desert far to the east, and by midforenoon I arrived at our home in Prosser.

My elation over the transaction I had made was of brief duration. Within a few days I learned that the government's title to the land on which I had filed was in question. The Federal grant of every odd-numbered section to the railroads extended for the distance of twenty miles on each side of their right of way. For some reason there had been an extension of railroad rights to the even-numbered sections in this area where my claim was located. This was contested by stockmen, squatters, and homesteaders. At the time when I filed on this property the case had not been adjudicated and there was still some prospect that the claim of the railroads would be set aside and the homesteaders would be granted title to their holdings. I, being new and green in the country, knew nothing of this situation. Some of my new friends were aware of it but true to the slogan of the frontier —Let the buyer beware—they kept their mouths shut. So did the Federal Land Officer at Cleveland. He stated later that he had asked the person who had sold the relinquishment whether he had informed me of the situation and upon his assurance that he had done so the deal was allowed to go through. This was a bitter disappointment to me!

25

Sometime within the next year the court upheld the claims of the railroads and all the prospects of a home in that part of the country vanished. So had the first money I had earned and saved. Then it seemed an irredeemable misfortune but as I look at it now it was one of the best investments I ever made. Those parasites that peddled gold bricks or offered patches of blue sky for sale were forever barred as far as I was concerned. When one of them appeared on the horizon I shied away from him like a horse from an open well and sounded the alarm whenever it appeared that they were closing in on a prospective buyer to relieve him of his money.

However, I had two cows and a calf, some lumber, fence posts, wire, and other chattels that were included in the deal. This made it necessary for me to return to the place for an inventory of my belongings and for a sale of the property. A doctor from Portland, Oregon, who had a winter cabin on some land he held, kindly bought what I had to sell. He and his wife lived in one of the most primitive shacks in the country and were so happy to be away from the crowded streets during a few months when the desert was in its best mood, and when the coastal cities and towns hung most of the time in a mist and fog.

It was during this trip that I had my first encounter with the eccentricities of this expanse of wasteland and learned how harsh and cruel the forces of nature can be. It was a pleasant morning when I left home for the thirty-five-mile ride to the homestead. It was an eventful trip. Everything was so new to me. The day was balmylike and cooler than usual. By this time the sheepmen were gone and the spring roundup was over. I arrived at my destination in good time, transacted what business there was, and was ready to return home the next morning. I spent a few hours that evening with the family that lived by the spring. They would have been our neighbors had not our deal fallen through. I then rode a mile or so up the coulee to the corral where I pulled the saddle off my horse, gathered up what feed there was left from the roundup, cooked my meal over a sagebrush fire, and lay down in a corner of the enclosure to sleep.

The next morning I was up early, prepared my breakfast, and got ready for the return trip home. When I reached the cabin by the spring I found the folks already astir, waiting for another opportunity to visit. At this time of the year places like this were lonely. Most of the people were gone and all through the long, hot summer months time hung monotonously on the hands of those who "stayed by the stuff." When I left them I was strongly urged to carry water with me. Since my ride of the day previous was so comfortable and pleasant I did not consider it necessary to encumber myself with one of their water bags, and planned to travel dry.

However, I tarried longer with my newly found friends than I had expected, and when I left the sun had already risen considerably above the horizon. I had not been on the way long until I saw what was happening. The sun came up with a sweltering heat. In the shimmering atmosphere, which one could see moving, the vegetation and life of the plains took on all kinds of grotesque forms. Bands of horses in the distance at one moment looked like trees walking while at the next they appeared greatly elongated and distorted into all sorts of shapes. The sagebrush, that denizen of the desert, which for ages has defied wind and heat and drought, assumed all kinds of hideous and deceitful forms. The sun kept getting hotter as it rose in the sky and after an hour or so the first breath of hot wind, heated by its long journey across the desert, struck me; at first in intermittent gusts, then in settled and continuous waves.

I began to realize that I had a hard trip ahead of me. The intense heat and the hot, dry, ashy dust that rose out of the footsteps of my saddle horse hung over and around me like a stifling blanket. Now and then a sharp puff of hot

27

wind swept it away, but before I had gone many rods, I was enshrouded again. I was becoming intensely thirsty. My mouth and throat became burningly dry, down into my lungs, it seemed—I had never been so thirsty! But it was too late now to return and pick up a bag of water. The only way out was to press on as rapidly as possible and try to get to the other side of the mountain where just over the crest there was a spring at the base of a large rock.

I looked for some signs of life but there were none except now and then a band of horses, which at first sight of me made their getaway and all that I saw was just another trail of dust. Everywhere there was a bleak, barren waste. What the day before had looked so restful and satisfying—even enchanting—had suddenly turned into a cauldron of heat and dust and ashes. What life there was had intuitively hidden itself away in the shadows of the coulees and buttes and rocks by such waters as it only knew.

By this time my thirst was becoming so intense that I began to wonder whether it might be worth while to turn off the trail and look for water. Perhaps in some coulee, I thought, there might be a spring which had been overlooked. But then what of common sense and judgment I had left came to my rescue and told me that such a venture would be worse than folly. All the tales of desert tragedies now came to my mind and I became almost afraid of myself. Would my judgment remain with me I wondered, or would I lose control of myself and begin to wander and roam and finally lose the trail and become swallowed up in the depth of these deep expanses? Others have done so, I recalled. But the crumpled hills of Horseheaven lay between me and water and home and were the compass to guide me on my way when everything else should fail.

I remembered that the previous day I had passed a cabin and now I recalled that I saw a pump beside it. Perhaps there was a well or cistern filled with water—maybe stale—

28

where I could refresh myself. So I hurried on. My throat was becoming so dry that it pained me; the heat and wind were intense and my thirst was growing all the time.

Looking into the distance, I saw what appeared like sheets of water, beautiful lakes, some so distinct and clear that the reflection of the sagebrush on the banks could be seen. Again and again I was tempted to ride in that direction and see if perhaps after all these mirages were not mirages, but instead real places of refreshment. But I knew better than to spend time and energy chasing after these will-o'-the-wisps that lure men on to death and are responsible for the bleaching bones of thousands that are strewn along the highways of the desert. I knew they were delusions, things that appeared to be close by, but like the end of a rainbow, they were always beyond. To a thirsty man whose mouth and throat were parched by the hot wind and irritated by the ashy dust, they looked inviting and at times very tempting but they were dangerous visions behind which lurked the powers of death. This I was aware of; so I restrained myself and kept going toward the hills.

As I rode along the lonely cabin, the only one in all that region, again came to my mind and the thought of the pump beside it gave me hope. Perhaps this settler had put down a well. If so, he had gone deep. Or perhaps it was a cistern which he filled with water that he hauled from springs, and there might be enough left so that I could quench my thirst. I hurried on as fast as I could and finally reached the place, which was entirely deserted. No doubt this man had been lured to this spot by some fake real-estate man and when he discovered what had happened to him, he did the wisest thing for anyone to do, that is, to leave as soon as he could. I reached the pump and found the handle locked, and search as I would, I could not find the key nor devise a way of prying it loose. I tried to break the lock. I did everything I could think of to unfasten it but it held firm.

I wondered what kind of man this unlucky fellow was that he should lock his pump or put his well into an unusable condition so that others could not get a little water when they were almost frantic for a drink. Why a man should deny another the right to anything he possessed in this forlorn, forsaken, dreary, dusty waste is more than I could understand. Especially so in a country where doors are never locked and a person is expected to stop and help himself to what he needs whether people are at home or not. Why on earth didn't he take his old pump along or why didn't he fill up the well if he didn't want it used! As I rode along I gave him a piece of my mind which he luckily never heard. Later I learned that the cistern was empty and that if I had succeeded in getting the handle loose, I would have gained nothing.

After spending precious time in vain, I saw there was nothing to do but to hasten on as fast as I could. My head was beginning to ache and I felt almost too sick to move. I brushed the dust from the nostrils of my horse, climbed into the saddle, and rode on. There were still miles and miles between me and water and more burning heat and wind. I wondered what would become of me. I had read that men become crazed from thirst and roam over the country in search of water until they drop in exhaustion and perish. Would I be able to hold on to the trail or would I follow after the delusions around me and perish? I knew my horse would take me home if I let her have the rein. Then I wondered whether I would do that or whether I could stay with her if I wanted to.

While in this state of mind there came to me a vague recollection of something I had heard from the Bible about "rivers of water in a dry place, . . . [and] the shadow of a great rock in a weary land." Again and again these words came to me. No doubt it was a land such as this of which the writer spoke—the barren wind-blown plains that lay between Palestine, the home of the prophet, and the mountains of Sinai or the hills of Moab.

I rode on and on. Sometimes I thought the hills were getting closer, then they appeared farther away than ever. But I kept on with but one thought in mind—to make the rock on the other side where I knew water was to be had. There I could quench my thirst and wallow in the stream and lie in the shadow of the shrubs and hide myself from the wind.

Finally I passed over the crest and began the steep descent. My throat was dry as though it had been baked, my tongue was parched and stuck to the roof of my mouth, but I had made my goal and was safe. I drew up alongside the rock, dismounted, and staggered over to the spring where I dipped up the water with my hat and threw it over my body. Then I stooped and drank. How sweet it tasted! But my stomach rebelled. I drank again with the same result. Then I lay down in the gathering shadows around the little pool where the bushes grew, in which birds sang in the morning and in the coolness of the evening. My head throbbed with pain; my body ached all over and I soon fell asleep. When I awoke the sun was low in the sky, and the hot wind had ceased to blow. The cooling evening air which always follows the setting sun had already sprung up. My horse was still standing by me. My muscles ached and my body was sore, but I managed to get back into the saddle and in a few hours I was safe at home.

A man shall be as an hiding place from the wind,
And a covert from the tempest;
As rivers of water in a dry place,
As the shadow of a great rock in a weary land.

This message from Isaiah, Israel's most gifted orator, is the one that rode with me across the desert that hot, thirsty day.

31

These are the gardens of the desert—
This the rugged, boundless, wild expanse
For which the speech of man has found no name.

IV

Moving to the Homestead

Sunflower Flat as it was known to stockmen, or Columbia Flat as it became known to later settlers, lay high above the lordly Columbia River that rolled past on its way to the Pacific Ocean. Years before Bryant, in his poem "Thanatopsis," had made mention of the place:

"Where rolls the Oregon and hears no sound save his own dashing" —this is it!

It was to this place that we came in quest of health and home after the loss of the claim on which I had earlier filed in the Horseheaven country.

For centuries this land was unoccupied except for roving bands of Indians and a few settlers along the river. Little settlements persisted at Waluke where the government maintained a weather station, at Muir's Landing, Ringold Bar, and at Holt's. At each of these places were located corrals where stockmen corraled during the roundup. At such times there was plenty of activity but when the rodeo moved on everything became quiet once more.

But long before the white people came this was the fishing and hunting ground of the Nez Perce Indians who roved from beyond the Snake River on the south to the Okanogan country on the north. They were Chief Joseph's people, a peaceable tribe, which was well governed by their able leader and wise and capable statesman, whose heart broke when the government took away their domain and confined them within the narrow boundaries of a reservation.

When the information spread that this section was to be placed under irrigation the railroad lands were quickly bought up by real-estate dealers and the government lands were as quickly taken up by homesteaders. Men and women left their occupation, their profession, or their business to follow the lure of fortune, hoping to stake out a claim, live on it the briefest possible time that would enable them to secure title, prove up and secure a deed from the government, turn on the water, and then sell the property and leave with a pocketful of money. In all of this they were eminently successful with the exception of turning on the water and leaving with a pocketful of money. Those two factors never materialized.

We joined this motley array, hoping to find our pot of treasure, not at the rainbow's end but on Columbia Flat, where I strove above all else to find in the quietness of these wide spaces a balm for my failing physique by breathing the magic ozone of the desert and feeding on other life-giving elements which we were told lurked here. These were dreams that filled my mind as I rode over the country eight months before to locate the corners of our claim. Little did I think, then, that a sojourn in these parts would be more than a holiday and that one who chooses to isolate himself from the haunts of civilization, miles from railroads or postal service, must be ready to pay the costs. Neither did I think that in spite of the hardships one would be compelled to undergo, he would become so attached to this solitude as to

34

make him loath to leave the place when the time came to do so.

When the month of June came, we had sold our home in Prosser and were ready to move. It was planned that I should take what possessions we had across the country by wagon and get things in readiness to live. My wife and little son were to follow some time later and I was to meet them at the station some twenty miles from our holdings and bring them to our new abode.

The morning on which I began the trip was the beginning of one of those beautiful western days that made a person feel strong and ready to undertake any task. The breezes were soft and balmy and the sky was blue and beautiful. The first few miles led through irrigated fields and orchards where the sent of the new-mown hay was fresh and the rows and rows of nicely cultivated trees testified of thrifty ownership and diligent labor. The country beyond was bleak and barren, except for the sagebrush and some spring flowers which the recent rains had awakened. Here the meadow lark sang his sweetest song to the solitary passers-by and one wondered what there was in this lonely place that made him sing unless it was the freshness of the morning air or the great, blue mountains—some with silver tops—that rose to the north and west.

It was my intention to make the Denning's ranch by noon the first day where I planned to feed and water. By evening I hoped to be able to make Benson's horse ranch on the other side of the Rattlesnake Mountains, where I could camp for the night at one of the springs from which some tracts of alfalfa were irrigated. Here I could also find feed for the team. As for lodging for myself, the canopy of the Western heavens was sufficient during the month of June when the breezes whisper one to sleep and the twinkling stars, like loving eyes, watch over one all the night long.

But the day was warm. By the time I reached the sheep

ranch it was past noon and the greater part of the trip still lay ahead of me. As soon as possible I started again and made my way up the winding trail. Without any incident worth mentioning I reached the summit just as the sun was sinking behind the blue peaks to the west. I stopped and stood up in my wagon. I was far from the haunts of man with nothing but the works of God about me. What wonder! What solitude! Here I stood on the height of those hills upon which I had so often looked and wondered what lay beyond. Now I was in the midst of them! Below me there were valleys and plains that stretched on and on to where the sun rose and north to where the Columbia cut its way through the Saddle Mountains. Before me along the trail lay deep, dark canyons and gullies through some of which the road would lead me. Away off to the east and far below me I saw the horse ranch—a patch of green—which from where I was looked like a garden plot, an oasis in the desert. Somewhat closer I saw another green spot which I had to reach in order to find feed and water and a camping place for the night.

The descent on the steep, rocky slopes was worse than I had anticipated. There were places where from my seat I looked down hundreds of feet to the floor of coulees and valleys. At times I drove with the lines wrapped around my arms or in my teeth, while I hung on the brake lever with both hands and pulled with all my might, and yet the wagon pushed up on the team until it looked as though the whole outfit might go over the embankment and land in a heap on the rocks far below.

The trail through these canyons was hard to follow. The beds were rocky and the track indistinct. From the mountaintop the camping place had not looked far away, but I had been going down the hill, through the hollows, and up the inclines until it seemed I had traveled miles and spent hours and yet the elusive alfalfa fields were not within reach.

Darkness had now set in and I was on the brink of another canyon. It looked so foreboding that I hesitated to enter. I could only guess what might happen in going through. There was the danger of missing the trail and going down over one of the ledges to death or perhaps worse—to be bruised and crippled, and lay, for what length of time nobody knew, until someone would pass that way. Or I might miss the trail and get into some narrow gorge from whence it would be impossible to extricate one's self in the night and possibly not in the daytime without a lot of trouble. I almost decided to camp dry until morning, but I knew what that would mean to my team. We had had no water since noon and unless I made it to the spring, we would not have any until morning. This made me bold to venture again. I entered the shadows once more and got safely through and continued on. I lighted my way through the coulees with matches; on the top the sagebrush guided me. I felt lost in the desert! There was no human being within reach and nothing to guide me except the stars and the dark five points of the Rattlesnakes, which I could distinguish against the sky line. Only the coyote with his plaintive cry spoke to me and warned me with a comfortless message that he was out looking for his midnight meal.

I recalled that people say that all things come to those who persevere and that success comes when it is least expected. These are good copybook maxims but I was so tired, and almost faithless in anything that man had told me, that platitudes such as these meant but little to me now and afforded me small consolation. Had they not told me that I could easily make the Big Rattlesnake Spring by dark? And here it was long after sunset, and I was, nobody knew, how far from my destination. Didn't people tell me that the road was good? and here for hours I had bounced up and down in my wagon, and walked and stumbled, then bounced again, until my body was sore, my temper was hanging by a mere thread, my faith was shaken, and my confidence shattered. I was almost ready to say that "all men are liars." In fact, when I saw the little junipers along the hillsides I was reminded of what Elijah did in the day when his confidence in men was low and I was about to give up too.

Just then when the gloom seemed deepest, I was almost sure that I saw a tree against the sky line. I knew that here in this country trees grow only by the streams or springs or along irrigation ditches. With hope renewed I drove on and suddenly my outfit came up against a fence, and behold! here was the alfalfa field which I had so much longed for. When I opened the gate I stepped into water to my ankles. Never since I was a little boy, playing in the puddles along the road, had I been so happy to have my shoes full of water. Suddenly my troubles had disappeared.

The next morning I was awake with the dawn. During the night the horses had filled themselves with the lush alfalfa. There was water aplenty. After a hastily prepared breakfast I drove to the ranch house at the lower spring, and then on to the last watering place where I spent the rest of the day in the little Eden among the shrubs and bushes and flowers which nature had planted there. How I longed to stay and rest a while! Here the birds who nested in the desert came for water when the sun was hot, and around the pool that was cooled by the flowing spring the horses of the range loitered through the heat of the day, until the shadows from the mountains flooded the landscape. Then they took up their pilgrimage to the back side of the desert in quest of food. How loath I was to leave the restfulness and comfort of this little paradise! Since then I have never read Psalm 104:10-12 but that this little scene comes to my mind and I try to relive again the experience of that day when life seemed so long and I felt so strong— strong enough to match wits and strength with the desert.

He sendeth the springs into the valleys,
Which run among the hills.
They give drink to every beast of the field:
The wild asses quench their thirst.
By them shall the fowls of the heaven have their habitation,
Which sing among the branches.

Psalm 104:10-12

When the coolness of the evening came I started on the last lap of the journey to the river. The remaining twenty miles to the Columbia were level, with outcroppings of basaltic rock, but there are no coulees nor gullies to mar the way. Sometime during the night when the moon was riding the crest of the Rattlesnakes I stopped at the foot of Gable Mountain, a bleak mass of igneous rock. For unknown centuries, yea, for unknown and unmeasured ages it has defied the wind and storms that swept about its head and the heat and cold that gnawed hopelessly at its massive form. It's a shelter in the time of storm and a resting place in a weary land.

I reached the Columbia, that wild torrent, when the sun rose. Like the Jordan of Joshua's day "it was out of its banks at the harvest time." There is a saying: "When the snows of the mountains melt, the river goes mad!" A call to the ferryman brought the wheezy, chuggy craft back from the White Bluffs side to where I was. I was soon across the mile-wide stream and after a difficult ascent up the bluffs, four to five hundered feet high, I found my way to the place where we were to spend three and one-half years of our lives.

Within a few days my wife's brother and I were on the way to the railroad for lumber for the new cabin. When it was completed the trip was made again to meet my family. Riding over the dusty miles was a new experience to them, but the trail led to our home in the land of our dreams, so full of hopes, so laden with hardships, and so rich with experience!

Cursed be the hand that scalps the reputation of the dead.

Chief Joseph

V

Chief Joseph's Land

The year before our arrival at Prosser, Washington, Joseph, the great chief of the Nez Perce Indians, died. At that time this event meant little to us. But a year later when we moved to our holdings on the Columbia River we discovered that we were settling in part of what was once the vast territory, grazing and hunting grounds, of that noted Indian leader, counselor, and statesman. His father like him had borne the same name—Chief Joseph. Like his son, he was also known as a man of wisdom, judgment, and honor—one who always sought peace for his followers. He was deeply interested in the welfare of his people who during his rule roamed over what is now Eastern Oregon, Washington, and Northern Idaho. They even ventured into the plains of Montana at certain seasons of the year to replenish their stock of supplies from the buffalo herds that grazed on the grasslands of the prairie.

Young Joseph was born in 1840 and according to tradition he was named In-mut-too-yah-lat-lat, which being interpreted means: Thunder Rolling over the Mountain—a beautiful name drawn from their wild surroundings. How well I recall the rumblings in the distant ranges that stood high above the lowlands which lay at their feet. His father died in 1872 and young Thunder-Rolling-over-the-Mountain became his successor and assumed his name, Chief Joseph.

The Nez Perces are said to have been very religious, worshiping their Great Spirit, in which, if one may judge from their practices during our sojourn within their territory, were involved the sun and the moon and the earth which gave them their living. They believed that the Creator had set up the order of the earth in a proper way and that it was wrong to disrupt it by plowing up the soil as the white man did in order to obtain grains and foods other than what nature provided. In the spring when the days began to lengthen they had their ceremonial exercises in which they welcomed the return of the Celestial Traveler who was coming to bring back to them the warmth of the summer, to make their land fruitful and fill the streams with water as the snows of the mountains melted. From those great hills and plains and rivers they drew the fruits, the meats, and the fish for their daily needs.

It has been mentioned that they were a peaceable people. The early travelers who had met the fierce Sioux, the Apaches, the Blackfeet, the Cheyennes, and others who were warlike and treacherous, were impressed with the gentle and friendly attitude of the Nez Perces.

The first contact these Indians had with the whites came through their dealings with the early traders—the French-Canadian **voyageurs**—who were scattered over the Northwest collecting furs from the natives in exchange for firearms, ammunition, blankets, and trinkets. The results of these meetings were not so good because these simplehearted children of nature soon discovered that the men with whom they bartered did not always tell the truth. Nor were they always honest. They drank firewater and tried to sell it to the Indians or trade it for their furs and wares, and in other ways took advantage of them.

Their next contacts were more favorable. Lewis and Clark were then making their famed exploration venture to the Pacific Coast. En route they found a Nez Perce woman who had been captured by the Plains Indians and helped her get back to her own people. She was treated so kindly by these white strangers that when they later met up with her tribe they were warmly received. This acquaintance-ship increased their confidence so much that when the explorers decided to proceed to the Pacific in boats they left their horses and equipment in the custody of Chief Joseph and his tribesmen. When they returned to claim their possessions they found everything in order with nothing wanting.

There is the fascinating story that has been retold again and again about the long trip of the four Indians who were sent to St. Louis, Missouri, in quest of the white man's religion and the Bible. They came from the Nez Perces. From some source they had received something that made them want this Book and someone to teach them. The arrival of this delegation created a great deal of interest in church circles. People were deeply stirred and it is said that ministers and pulpit orators cashed in on this event to stimulate and promote missionary interest throughout the country. The representatives of this commission bore typical Indian names, Black or Speaking-Eagle, Man-of-the-Morning, Rabbit-Skin-Leggins, and No-Horns-on-His-Head. The first two died while in St. Louis, and the last one on his way home. The only one who survived the trip was Rabbit-Skin-Leggins.

As a result of this incident Dr. Marcus Whitman, Rev.

Samuel Parker, and Rev. H. H. Spaulding were sent forth as missionaries in 1836. The story of their journey and their adventures among this tribe is one of the most thrilling in the history of missions. Whitman finally located at what is now Walla Walla, Washington, and Spaulding settled at Lapwai, Idaho. As a result of the work of Spaulding it is said that at one time practically the whole of the Nez Perces had accepted Christianity, and Chief Joseph, the father of the tribe, located at Wallowa, Oregon, became an ardent disciple of the newly espoused faith.

As usual the coming of the white man to take up lands for cultivation created disturbances among the original occupants. During the rush to the new country that lay between the Rocky Mountains and the Pacific some of the immigrants stopped in the valleys of Idaho, Eastern Washington, and Oregon. The Nez Perces had stock on the range and profited by this influx of settlers. Their horses, which had been crossed with the best sires available, were in demand.

Along about the middle of the nineteenth century the white population had increased so much that they petitioned the governor of the Oregon Territory to establish reservations for the Indians and move them off the open country. Rather than to have war or trouble Old Chief Joseph consented. As a result of this agreement he and his people were given a large tract which embraced what has now become Eastern Oregon, Eastern Washington, and Northern Idaho. This land, it was agreed, should be theirs forever. In return for this concession the government was to pay them, in annual installments, over a million dollars. Other stipulations in the contract guaranteed them exclusive possession of the wide expanse reserved for them. The whites were to be prohibited from entering the Indian domain. The sale of liquor within its boundaries was forbidden and made illegal by Federal authorities, and in addition the red men

44

were to have exclusive hunting and fishing rights within their territory.

However good the terms of this treaty appeared the question was not permanently settled. The white population continued to grow. The government did not honor all its agreements with the Indians. The cash payments which were to have been made regularly were never fully paid. Ranchers and stockmen crossed into the reservation and established themselves in business. Miners came by the thousands with the discovery of gold, and ignored all the rights of the natives. They abused the Indian women, killed off the game, sold liquor to the red men, and in other ways treated them as though they had no rights or as though they were not a people.

The tensions grew, and by 1863 the situation had become so serious that the Washington government ordered the negotiation of a new treaty. However unsatisfactory this was to the Nez Perces it was signed by the chief of one of its tribes who did so without the approval of the council or the consent of the other chiefs. Most of the tribes accepted this act but the venerable Joseph together with the leaders of three other tribes refused to recognize it. When confronted with the question of his attitude Joseph replied: "I have kept my faith; let the whites keep theirs."[1] He warned his people, "Never give up the land where your fathers are buried." The old patriarch refused to be bribed with presents with which the government agents would have smothered him, saying to his son, Thunder-Rolling-over-the-Mountain, "If you take their presents they will say we have sold our lands to them."

The four nontreaty bands refused to vacate the portion of their territory which had been taken from them by the recent agreement and continued to roam over it with their herds of horses and cattle to the annoyance of the settlers. The pressures increased as the whites encroached more deeply upon the Indian holdings. Finally in 1868 they were ordered to leave their country and move to the reservation which the government had set apart for them. This they refused to do. Old Chief Joseph, it is said, became so enraged over the treatment they were receiving that he destroyed the copy of the Bible given him by his friend, Rev. Spaulding, and he together with all of his followers renounced Christianity and turned to their own gods. What a pity that something so beautiful as the Gospel should be so poorly lived by its adherents and propagators as to cause its repudiation by these children of the wilderness who had once accepted it!

For years this great leader had witnessed and endured all kinds of injustices and misrepresentations at the hands of the government agents. He and his people suffered abuses, wrongs, trickery, deceit, and broken promises at the hands of the settlers and the miners that flowed into the country. He saw some seventy thousand dollars of money, which belonged to his tribe, disappear at the hands of unscrupulous employees at the agency. He endured all of this rather than take his people into war, and always turned a deaf ear to suggestions of violence. As far as is known neither he nor his people had up to that time killed a white person. This is more than can be said of the intruders, who constantly encroached upon the rights and possessions of Joseph and his followers. Many an Indian fell at the hands of these contenders for the soil and many an Indian woman suffered the outrages, indignities, and abuses inflicted by these invaders of their domain.

Death came to the old chief in 1872. As he lay dying amid the monotonous beating of the tom-tom and the sound of the shuffling feet of the medicine dance, he called his son to his side and gave him his final charge:

"My son," he said, "this old body is returning to my mother earth, and my spirit is going very soon to see the

46

Great Spirit Chief. Give ear to me. When I am gone, think of your country. You are the chief of these people. They look to you to guide them. Always remember your father never sold his country. You must stop your ears when you are asked to sign a treaty selling your home. A few more years and white men will be all around you. They have their eyes on this land. My son, never forget my dying words. This country holds your father's body. Never sell the bones of your father and mother."[2]

Upon his death, young Joseph—Thunder-Rolling-over-the-Mountain—found himself at the head of a people without a land except for such as their exploiters were willing to grant them. The vast territory which had been theirs for centuries and which they had steadfastly refused to leave was taken from them. He inherited from his ancestor not only a position and a people, but a very troublesome situation that was soon to burst into flames. The young Indians, though not inclined to be warlike, were not willing to stand by and see their lands go into other hands, which could only mean confinement within the bounds of a reservation allotted to them by the government. And when once they were sure that their rights could not be maintained by peaceable negotiations they, against the counsel of their leader, resorted to all the means which they knew in order to protect and defend their possessions. This eventually led to warfare with all the atrocities that followed in its wake.

In 1877 General Howard who had long been their friend was ordered by the government at Washington to round up those who ignored the Treaty of 1863, and forcibly, if necessary, place them on the reservation. The general then called a council of the Nez Perce chiefs which Joseph attended reluctantly. In the discussions that followed he proved himself to be the equal of his illustrious father.

"If we ever owned this land," he said in defense of his position, "we own it still, for we never sold it. In treaty councils the commissioners have claimed that our country has been sold to the government. Suppose a white man should come to me and say, 'Joseph, I like your horses, and I want to buy them.' I say to him, 'No, my horses suit me; I will not sell them.' Then he goes to some neighbor and says to him, 'Joseph has some good horses. I want to buy them but he refuses to sell.' My neighbor answers, 'Pay me the money, and I will sell you the horses.' The white man returns to me and says, 'Joseph, I have bought your horses, and you must let me have them.' If we sold our lands to the government, that is the way they were bought."[3]

This was not only good logic but it was downright common sense. However, his reasoning was unavailing and his words received scant consideration.

During the heat of the conference General Howard ordered the arrest of an Indian priest, Too-hul-hul-suit, whose attitude was very defiant. He consumed a lot of time by what the general considered worthless talk. His commitment to prison caused considerable excitement among his followers and intensified the feeling that was already running high. A few days later Joseph promised to go to the reservation in order to secure the release of his spiritual counselor and adviser. He still wanted to avoid bloodshed and recommended a peaceable transfer to their new home. He agreed to leave his beloved Wallowa—"Land of Winding Waters"—in Northeastern Oregon, the place where he lived during his boyhood, and the land where his father's bones were buried, rather than become involved in warfare. But the other chiefs and the younger men thought otherwise.

They were given thirty days to round up their five thousand horses and one thousand head of cattle which were scattered over a wide range. Anyone who is familiar with the country knows that even now such an undertaking would be impossible. It was much more so then.

While the Indian chiefs were sitting in council, other things were happening. A young buck killed a settler who some time earlier had slain his father. Until then it is said they had never killed a white man, nor fought a neighboring tribe. Referring to this incident later Joseph is reported to have said, "I would have given my own life if I could have undone this act." But it was too late. Other killings followed and before the fracas was over eighteen whites had "bitten the dust." Joseph still counseled peace but his tribesmen clamored for revenge. The conflict was on and the Great Chief decided to stay with his people.

Then began the bitter struggle—the only war ever waged between the Nez Perces and the United States Army. The months that followed were filled with tragedy and all the hardships and sufferings that follow in the wake of warfare. On the day when the battle began, Chief Joseph's wife gave birth to a daughter. On that memorable day months later when he rode to the tent of Generals Miles and Howard to surrender she was the only child he had left. During the last days of the struggle his only other remaining child, a daughter, was lost in the confusion of the battle. Some time later she was restored to him.

On the one side of this conflict was the United States Army in command of officers trained and schooled in the arts of warfare and seasoned by years of service in the field during the Civil War. On the other side was a young Indian chief untaught in military tactics, unskilled and inexperienced, who knew nothing about war. But he proved himself a remarkable leader and an able strategist. So much so that army men, trained at West Point, who had long and creditable records of service during the struggle between the states, found themselves outwitted and outgeneraled again and again. Joseph had only some three hundred and fifty men but he had with him also, all through his brilliant campaign, the wives and the children of his warriors to carry with him, to protect and feed. Besides that he had the eleven hundred horses and whatever cattle he had salvaged when they were ordered to move to the reservation. General Howard had only his soldiers and their provisions to concern himself with.

Beset by the army under the command of able military officers, their blood-covered trail led them over two thousand miles through Idaho, Wyoming, and northward through Montana, over some of the wildest and most rugged country in the West, to within a short distance of the Canadian border.

Then General Miles took charge of the army. The cold northern winter was at hand. Food was scarce. Chief Joseph's people were inadequately clothed and had but few blankets. They were beginning to scatter through the hills in search of protection. The children and the old people were freezing to death. Joseph's own brother, Ollicut, and his faithful and dependable associate, Chief Looking-Glass, had both been killed. Of the three hundred and fifty men he had when the war started, only eighty-seven were left, of which forty were wounded.

Being hard pressed by General Miles who was about to join forces with General Howard, Joseph received two Indians—Nez Perces—who were attached to General Howard's staff and served the army as interpreters. One of them was Captain John. They were sent into the Nez Perce camp to ask for Joseph's surrender and informed him of the general's assurance of good treatment. These emissaries of peace urged the Indians to give up the struggle. Upon the promise that they could return to their beloved Lapwai in Idaho, unless higher authorities ordered otherwise, the chief decided to give up and commit himself and the remnant of his followers to the custody of the army. When this word was passed along, White-Feather, the only other surviving chief, together with his family and some of his band, fled into Canada. This left Joseph with only women and children and a few able-bodied men. Later in the day Captain John and his companion returned to headquarters of Generals Miles and Howard with this message from the chief:

"Tell General Howard that I know his heart. What he told me before—I have it in my heart. I am tired of fighting. Our chiefs are killed. Looking-Glass is dead. Too-hul-hul-suit is dead. The old men are all dead. It is the young men now who say 'yes' or 'no.' He who led the young men, Ollicut [Joseph's brother], is dead. It is cold and we have no blankets. The little children are freezing to death. My people—some of them—have run away to the hills, and have no blankets and no food. No one knows where they are—perhaps freezing to death. I want to have time to look for my children, and see how many of them I can find; maybe I shall find them among the dead. Hear me, my chiefs; my heart is sick and sad. I will no more fight the white man."[4]

What an eloquent, touching, heart-searching plea for consideration this was! It was nearly sunset when Joseph, accompanied by five of his men, rode up to the tent where General Miles and General Howard were waiting to receive him. With hand uplifted he turned and looked across the snow fields into the closing day and said: "From where the sun now stands I will no more fight the white man for-ever!"[5] Then he dismounted with much grace and with great dignity passed his rifle, butt first, to General Miles as a token of his surrender. After this he turned, and walked to the tent that was provided for him.

The war with the Nez Perces was over. The promise he made that day was never broken. But their freedom was gone, and the destruction of Chief Joseph's tribe was almost complete. Their land which they so loved was lost and they would no more roam as happy children over the great expanses of mountains and valley and plain as they once had.

51

On the evening when he passed his rifle to General Miles he carried his head high like the noble son of the wild that he was. But his head drooped the next day as he sat watching his people file by into servitude. He counted as they went, one hundred and eighty-four women, one hundred and forty-seven children; and some fifty men of whom forty were wounded. Of the five thousand horses they had had on the range, they had succeeded in getting some eleven hundred head which together with more than a hundred saddles were given up on the day of their surrender. They were a people with nothing in their hands except unhonored agreements, broken promises, and lost hopes, and in their bosoms aching hearts—these children of the wilderness, victims of the white man's exploitation.

The promise of General Miles to return them to their home on the Snake River in their beloved Lapwai country with its mountains and valleys, which was received with such great joy, was all too soon turned into disappointment and sorrow.

Owing to the lateness of the season and the destitute condition of the people the following order was issued by General Howard who was then in command of the Department of the Columbia.

Headquarters, Department of the Columbia. In the Field, Battlefield of Eagle Creek near Bear-Paw Mountain, Montana.
October 7, 1877

Colonel Nelson A. Miles
Fifth Infantry
Commanding District of the Yellowstone

COLONEL:

On account of the cost of transportation of the Nez Perce prisoners to the Pacific Coast, I deem it best to retain them at some place within your district, where they can be kept under military control till next spring. Then unless you receive instructions from higher authority, you are hereby directed to have them sent under proper guard to my department, where I will take charge of them and carry out the instructions I have already received.

O. O. HOWARD
Brigadier-General, Commanding Department.[6]

It was then decided that they should spend the winter on the Tongues River in Montana. But when their case got into the hands of the politicos in the National Capital this remnant of a noble race became again the victims of a long list of agreements that were never kept. Instead of keeping them at the Tongues River as was the original plan they were sent to the Dakotas. From there, in spite of the pleadings of General Miles, they were shipped to Fort Leavenworth, Kansas. In their mountain homeland they drank the pure, cool, crystal clear water from the streams and springs. During their Kansas sojourn they dipped it from the muddy Missouri and lived in the miasma-laden flood plains along the river. The next summer they were again moved, this time into the hot, dry prairie lands of what was then Indian Territory, to whose climate they were strangers. During their stay there one hundred and fifty of them, together with all the newly born children, died.

The negotiations of this simplehearted, honest child of nature with Indian agents, politicians, and government officials were most disappointing and trying. In referring to these experiences, he says:

"I have heard talk and talk but nothing is done. Good words do not last long unless they amount to something. Words do not pay for my dead people. They do not pay for my country now overrun by white man. They do not protect my father's grave. They do not pay for all my horses and cattle. Good words will not give me back my children. Good words will not make good the promises of your war chief General Miles. Good words will not give my people good health and stop them from dying. Good words will not get

53

my people a home where they can live in peace and take care of themselves. I am tired of talk that comes to nothing."[7]

Then followed one more eloquent plea for himself and for his race. "Let me be a free man," he said, "free to travel, free to stop, free to work, free to trade where I choose, free to choose my teachers, free to follow the religion of my fathers, free to talk and think and act for myself and I will obey every law or submit to the penalty."[8]

Did ever anyone make a more simple and eloquent plea for freedom? Does it not seem like mockery that a people like the whites who claimed all these rights for themselves and gave their blood that they might enjoy those liberties should deny them to those who had occupied the soil for centuries?

After several more years of disappointment it was finally decided that the remnant that survived the hardship and suffering of the years since they gave up the struggle should be moved at last to their home in Idaho near the western border of the state, Lapwai. Chief Joseph, however, was not allowed to accompany them. He was assigned to the Colville Reservation in Northern Washington where he lived the rest of his days in a tepee. Although he had been given a house, he refused to occupy it.

Recognizing the wrong that had been done to this noble son of the mountain and desert and his people, the whites now tried to atone for their treatment of him by inviting him to their social functions and entertainments at which he was probably ill at home. They paid his traveling and other expenses to Eastern cities. They dined and tried to "wine" him at the Astor House, took him to football games and other activities in various parts of the country. Society received him royally but he was not impressed or affected except that his hurts may have become deeper. What could the floors—richly covered with deep-piled oriental rugs—of

Astor's palatial hotel mean to one who all his life had walked the leaf-carpeted halls of the forest or the grass-covered plains of his Idaho or Oregon home? Or what were the congestions of Fifth Avenue or similar places, where people smother in the rush, and the all too frequent inconsiderations and unkindnesses of the multitude, in comparison with the trails that lead to snow peaks, the tree-covered and flower-bedecked hills and plains, swept by the pure air of heaven?

At last one September evening in 1904, he died suddenly while walking near his tepee on the Colville Reservation. As we, my wife and I, remember it now, he was succeeded by Chief To-ma-na-wah. Old Chief Joseph was buried at Wallowa, but years afterward his body was moved to a beautiful spot overlooking the lake where a monument was raised over his remains. His son, Thunder-Rolling-over-the-Mountain, was permitted only once to visit this shrine. When he died he was laid to rest on the Colville Reservation where he spent his last years. His burial place is marked by a simple marble shaft, an empty remuneration for the wrongs and mistreatment he had suffered. In his later years, as in his death, he was honored and respected by all.

During our life on Columbia Flat we occasionally saw remnants of his tribe wander across the country. They were broken fragments of a goodly race, children that roamed over the wide spaces seeking food and sustenance. During the summer when the salmon came in from the sea and rushed hysterically up the rivers and streams to their spawning grounds, little groups of Indians with spears in their hands could be seen on horses riding the "riffles" as the rapids were called, catching the fish on their way up or down stream. Later when the waters teemed with the floating bodies of those that were bruised and broken on their way over the falls or the swift, rocky inclines, and floated down with the current, the Indians in their frail canoes were busy picking them up for food.

If one should have visited their camps, these same fish would have been seen hanging in the sun where they were dried for winter use. Often these wandering, unwanted children were also seen traveling in spring wagons, followed by their small bands of horses, going to the berry and hop fields on the coast. They evidently still had some stock on the range. Every roundup had one or more of their tribe in it to see that their colts received the proper brand and to make such disposition of their holdings as was desired.

But they were a wounded, disappointed, heartbroken people who found it difficult to take on the white man's ways or to submit to his wayward willfulness. Their great chief was spoken of with awe, almost with reverence, by the rivermen, the stockmen, and all who knew him except the settlers who dispossessed him and his people of their possessions. He was remembered for his peaceful inclinations, his honesty, kindness, and his virtue. In fact, his people as well as all Indians held to a higher type of morals than did most of the folks with whom they dwelt and dealt. He was an orator, statesman, a wise counselor, and a child of peace and justice, but his virtues were ignored, his honesty taken advantage of, and his wise counsels overruled. It is said that no Indian suffered greater injustice and abuse at the hands of the white people and deserved it less.

He was not only loved and respected for his moral qualities but his wisdom and shrewdness are acknowledged wherever he is known. His wise sayings were household words, not only among his own people but also among many of those who had known him. Some of his maxims were recalled by the settlers among whom we lived. In his article in the magazine entitled **True,** Robert E. Pinkerton quotes a few which were taken from a collection compiled by the **New York Sun**:

"When you can get the last word with an echo, you may have the last word with your wife."

56

"A big name often stands on small legs."

"Look twice at a two-faced man."

"Firewater ends in trembling fear."

"Cursed be the hand that scalps the reputation of the
dead."[9]

Noble proverbs are these! But what a pity that a people
who had in them so much that is good and who had progressed so much toward the right, who had even called for
the Book of books and teachers to teach them, should receive such treatment at the hands of the race that brought
it to them, as to cause them to renounce the faith they had
asked for and accepted! What a travesty upon a cause and
what a defeat it was to those who brought this tragic experience to pass in the life of one who said: "I would rather
give up my life than take my people to war."

[1] Wood, C. E. S., "Chief Joseph, The Nez Perce," *The Century Illustrated Magazine,* Vol. 128, Old Series, p. 135. London (in the library of
Goshen College, Goshen, Ind.).

[2] Hare, William H., "An Indian's View of Indian Affairs," *The North
American Review,* D. Appleton Co., New York, 1879, Vol. 128, p. 419.

[3] Wood, C. E. S., *Ibid.,* p. 135.

[4] Wood, C. E. S., *Ibid.,* p. 141.

[5] Authorities do not agree on the order of this dramatic statement.
General Wood includes it as part of the message which Joseph sent by
the interpreters. Joseph says that he made the statement when he gave
up his rifle. See *The North American Review,* Vol. 128, p. 429.

[6] Wood, C. E. S., *Ibid.,* p. 142.

[7] Hare, William E., *Ibid.,* p. 432.

[8] Hare, William E., *Ibid.,* p. 433.

[9] Pinkerton, Robert E., "The Indian Who Beat the U.S. Army," *True,*
The Man's Magazine, Vol. 32, April, 1953. Fawcall Publications, Inc.,
Greenwich, Conn., p. 54.

Lord, I've never lived where churches grow;
I've loved Creation better as it stood
The day you finished it so long ago,
And looked upon your work and called it good.

Just let me live as I've begun!
And give me work that's open to the sky;
Make me a partner of the wind and sun,
And I won't ask a life that's soft and high.

Make me as big and open as the plains;
As honest as the horse between my knees;
Clean as the wind that blows behind the rains;
Free as the hawk that circles down the breeze.

Just keep an eye on all that's done and said;
And right me when sometimes I turn aside;
And guide me on the long, dim trail ahead—
That stretches upward toward the Great Divide.

Author Unknown

VI

Knights of the Jingling Spurs

The saga of the Great Plains and the Great American Desert is but a continuation of the old controversy one reads about in the days of the patriarchs and before. It is the struggle against the wild elements of nature which these hardy and adventurous souls faced in their efforts to find water and grass for their herds and flocks. Those battles often took place around the springs, creeks, and rivers—watering places—without which the grasses became almost worthless and their animals could not survive. It was between the cattle and sheepmen, and later between the agriculturalists and the stockmen who contended for possession of the range, that the final contest was waged in order to decide who was to have possession of the land. The story, from its earliest appearance in history, is frequently filled with hardship and harshness and cruelty.

Cain was a stockman and built an enclosure—perhaps a corral—to keep his herds together. Abraham's flocks grazed over the plains of Northern Mesopotamia and later on the hills and in the valleys of Palestine. The quarrel between his herdsmen and those of Lot over the grasslands and watering places was surely not the first one, nor were such affairs always as amicably and considerately settled between the proprietors as was theirs. The feud over water and pasture again flared up at Beersheba when Abimelech's flocks crowded in upon Abraham's range. In Isaac's day he was forced from his grazing grounds by the Philistines who destroyed the wells which his father had dug. When he had digged new ones in the plains of Gerar he was driven from thence also and started over again at Rehoboth.

Jacob found his beloved Rachel by the watering trough in Haran. When he later took charge of his father-in-law's flocks he herded them along the grassy valleys of the Euphrates and no doubt far beyond into the wide steppes of Syria. Moses, a prince from the courts of Pharaoh, steeped in the learning of Egypt's schools, won the gratitude of Jethro, a priest of Midian, when he defended his daughter at the pools of Arabia, in the desert at the foot of Sinai. As a reward for his kindness he was taken into the priestly stockman's home and given a wife—Zipporah—from the daughters of the family. He like Jacob became the manager of his father-in-law's affairs and took care of his sheep for the next two score years. Through the milleniums of years that came and went their successors have ever followed the lure of new pasture lands which finally brought them to the last grazing frontier, the great open plains, the wide expanses and the deep wastes of North and South America.

The first more or less settled white occupants of the plateaus and plains of America were stockmen. The land was open and the range was free for such as were willing to endure the rigors of the wild and the loneliness of isolation for the remuneration and rewards that their occupation yielded them. Those who made this venture were hardy souls; brave, daring, adventurous, often crafty and cruel when their rights were infringed upon or their business interfered with. The occasion and the situation demanded such qualities. Among the great names that stand out as towering peaks above all the others are those of Charles Goodnight, John S. Chisum, Andrew Drumm, Jesse M. Chisholm, and John W. Iliff. They were not the earliest ones who occupied the range but among the greatest. These and others equally or less renowned who came earlier and later were members of the great fraternity of cattlemen that reaches back, as already noted, deeply into ancient times. They were the ones who turned the grasses of the wide spaces into meat for the markets of the world. Along with them came cattle companies financed and operated by foreign capital—Englishmen and Scotchmen who were located in foreign lands, and Americans who hailed from the cities of the eastern part of the United States. Their interest was drawn to the range lands for the profits which they hoped would accrue from such investments and ventures.

But the West held other attractions besides those of grazing and stock raising. The early discovery of gold and silver brought another class of men on the scene. They were the prospectors, miners, merchants, vendors of liquor, operators of gambling places, lurid women, and camp followers of all kinds who came to profit by the opportunities that were open to their trades, their vices and devices. Among them were criminals and fugitives from justice who fled the home community, gamblers, bad men and women, and bunko men of all kinds. The absence of the strong arm of the law and the sure but orderly judicial processes, the sparse population, the large territory and rough character of the society in general made this an attractive place for

61

people such as they. Besides this, the places where precious metal accumulates as it does around the mines and where movable wealth, such as cattle and horses that can be more or less easily transferred from one place to another and turned into money, is found are inviting.

It seems that the cattle and horsemen were the first to occupy the open lands. They considered their business a respectable one. They occupied the range and while they owned little of it, they claimed it all, or at least they insisted on their right to occupy it. When the sheepmen later invaded the country they met with opposition of the most bitter and vigorous kind. In some parts, as for example in Wyoming, it reached a stage of violence that is spoken of as the war between sheepmen and cattlemen. In other places it was no doubt just as bad. Hence the cattlemen and their cohorts looked with disdain upon the sheepmen and considered them as a people who were hardly a people. This was especially true of their attitude toward the men who followed the sheep across the range. I have known instances of where cowboys and buckaroos refused to ride in the same caboose with sheepherders when shipping stock to the market. The riding, roping, branding, and other duties that fall to the lot of the employees of the horse and cattle companies require a lot of intelligence and skill. By them it is generally thought that the herder requires little of either and that the long, lonely months they spend with their flocks of woollies have a tendency to make them peculiar. Even the owners share something of this attitude. Once, when I was a guest in the home of one of the proprietors of a large cattle and sheep company in Southwest Colorado, one of the party spoke up and said, "I guess a sheepherder has to know a good deal in order to herd sheep." To which the manager of the company drawled, "Yaas, he ought to know at least as much as the sheep."

62

The wide open range country was magnificent. For years the cattle and horses of the different companies drifted far and wide over the grazing grounds which were occupied in common and the stock of the different owners was distinguished by the brand it bore. Ranching establishments were often considerable distances apart and some effort was made by the management to keep their cattle from scattering too widely. Cowboys were continually on the alert easing alien critters off their range and throwing back those of their own to within the bounds of their territory.

When a section of the country became too crowded, some of the ranchers moved onward to new pastures and watering places. In the course of time some of the stockmen began to purchase large tracts of land on which to run their herds, and smaller operators took up part of the range. This precipitated some trouble.

Then, as is so often the case, something happened that greatly affected the ranching business. Joseph Glidden, a young man at De Kalb, Illinois, conceived the idea of making barbwire as a means of fencing fields and keeping livestock within or out of bounds. As the range in the West was becoming more crowded with cattle and an increasing number of ranchers came, some of the stockmen began to enclose their holdings. During the last decades of the 1800's the young manufacturer shipped trainloads of his product to Texas, Kansas, Colorado, and what is now Oklahoma and Wyoming and, in fact, to all the prairie states as well as to the farmers of the agricultural regions of the country.

This precipitated another struggle between cattlemen. Some contended for the open range. Others wanted their holdings fenced in. After years of wire cutting, bitter feuding, and fatalities, the barbwire men finally won. Today, except for some deeply isolated places or government reserves, stock roams within enclosed grazing grounds, some of which are immensely large.

The men who operated these cattle and horse ranches came from many points of the compass. Some were college bred, as, for example, John W. Iliff. He had been a student —perhaps a graduate of Delaware College—and followed the call of the cow country to become one of the princes of the cattle kingdom. He, himself, homesteaded a piece of land. His employees filed on claims which Iliff bought until he owned all the territory along the banks of the South Platte River for a distance of more than thirty-five miles. But his cattle grazed even beyond the bounds of his titled holdings for a hundred miles or more up and down the stream. The capitol of his little empire was located at Julesburg, Colorado. His cowpunchers, as they were called, were intensely loyal to him. They enforced his demands to the letter and guarded his rights with a jealousy and devotion that bordered on fanaticism. He, like a true son of the West, shared the hardships of ranch life with them. He braved the storms, rode fence if necessary, and ate and slept with his men at the sod way stations that were scattered along the border of his little kingdom.

John W. Chisolm was a half-breed whose father was a Scotchman and his mother a Cherokee Indian. From both his ancestors he inherited the best traits of their race which gave him a character that was eminently fitted to meet all the emergencies and exigencies that his business carried with it.

Jess Chisum, giant operator, finally settled at his famed South Springs Ranch in Texas where he established himself as one of the monarchs of the domain over which his stock roamed. The kind of men with which he surrounded himself indicates something of the situations which those of his type and occupation had to face. Among them, though not a part of his outfit, was Billy the Kid, one of the most lethal outlaws of his time.

Drumm was a German, who was once one of the big

ranchers but who operated in his later years at the selling end of the trail and added to his millions the profits of the commission business at the smelly stockyards of Kansas City.

The final contest for possession of the grazing lands of the West was with those who wanted to turn the prairie into farms or wheat ranches. This group was known as the nesters and consisted of people who took up the vacant land either by purchase or homesteading, broke the sod, and put the land under cultivation. This increased the problem of the stockmen. Little islands of grain in the midst of vast holdings of grazing land often made it impossible for the cattlemen to continue the earlier methods of handling their business. States enacted legislation dealing with the problem but brought no solution. Some of them by law held that the farmer must fence in his land and leave the open portions to the ranchers. Others seemingly favored the nester and said that the stockmen must do the fencing or be held liable for the damage their stock may do the farmer's crops. The controversy between these rivals became bitter in many places. The ranchers finally changed their method of operations and adjusted themselves to the situation and the dry farmers won the day. In some places their victory was justifiable. In other places it was a tragedy because good grasslands were turned into unprofitable agricultural ventures. The range was spoiled, the ground was broken, and the wind blew the soil away.

In the country where we lived this struggle was brief and never reached a critical stage. Most of those who took up land did not enclose it with barbwire. Those who did and tried dry farming soon abandoned all their effort and let the land revert to sagebrush and sheep grass.

Today the vast areas of the Columbia Flat are waiting for irrigation developments and in the meantime it is the winter home of sheepmen and the grazing ground for bands

65

of horses who escape the occasional roundups when "the Knights of the Jingling Spurs" gather for a brief fling at the past in this as in other places of the Old West that is going out—except for the dude ranches. How these old cow horses must chafe under the avoirdupois of the chattering females and the "heroic" males whose most serious purpose is to give their hide a sun tan while sweltering in the heat of their air-conditioned rooms in cactus land where they satisfy their appetites in dining rooms that have little resemblance to those where the rugged cow hands ate when they came in from the day's ride!

But better known to me than the cattlemen were the horsemen that rode the range that lies between the Rockies and the Cascades, in the sagebrush regions north of the Snake River. Here the Gable outfit, the Bensons, the Savages, the William Boys, and others of major and minor importance operated during the days of our sojourn in the desert. Here, too, we were brought in contact with a type of life that was paling before the encroachment of irrigation developments, the wheat ranchers and the homesteaders. In this section, too, we met up with the sheepmen—the Schlomers, the Dennings, and others whose flocks numbering tens of thousands and more were brought in from the mountain pastures to graze for the winter.

The operators of the ranches, horse or cattle, furnished the money, provided the business acumen, the thought and management for their spread. But they were helpless without the buckaroo or the cowboy. The lines of distinction between the two may not always be as clearly drawn as they were in the section of the country where we lived. There the former term applied to those who handle horses, and the latter to those who handle cattle. Here the buckaroo stood at the head of the scale. The "Sons of the Saddle" that rode for horses were considered the elite.

In our country—the sagebrush land—the cattle business

was almost nonexistent. Scarcity of watering places and the scant grasses were against the beef growers. Horses can go long distances to water, but cattle cannot. This then made the Columbia Flat and the surrounding lands a horse country where the buckaroo was at home. Like his kinsman, the cowboy, he was a hard riding man of the saddle, skilled with a rope and quick on the draw. He was perhaps not as loyal to his outfit as the cowpuncher, whose employment was more continuous throughout the year and who was a part of a larger body than was the employee of the horseman.

The question often arises, Where did these men come from? Were they born and reared in the desert and on the plains or did they come from other parts of the country? As I think of it now I recall how many of those whom I knew came from Texas, the Cherokee Strip, and from New Mexico. There they received their training in the hard school of experience when the country was untamed and wild. Many of them came from the southern highland states—Kentucky, Tennessee, and other sections in which feuding was common and where people still largely settled their own affairs, sometimes in a violent manner. These brought with them the spirit which they inherited from their ancestors, some of whom never were quite ready to accede to the government the powers which they considered theirs by right of the situations under which they lived.

On the range they were hard-working, dependable men, ordinarily sober, self-reliant, and loyal to their outfit. When, however, occasions such as delivery of stock brought them to the towns in groups they usually sought release from the tensions of loneliness by indulging in amusements and entertainment that in most communities would be considered quite unorthodox. Under the influence of liquor old scores were settled, ofttimes in a violent manner. Drinking, gambling, and carousing were common. On the long

67

trail drives that sometimes required months of time and patience the tension became high and bad feeling in the camp resulted in tragedy. While loading the chuck wagon for a long drive a newcomer saw the trail boss put a spade with the equipment and asked what they needed it for. He received the reply, "You kain't bury no cowpuncher without no spade."

In the places where large cattle ranches existed some of the men became practically a permanent part of the outfit they served. Many of them were untutored children of the wild with but little book learning—some with none—but they were deeply steeped in the lore of nature and were highly skilled in the arts of their business. When they spoke many of them violated every law of grammar and virtually slaughtered the language. But they were blissfully ignorant of their crime. Since motive constitutes an important element in guilt, they would likely have been acquitted at the bar of any judicial tribunal that functioned in their day. In recent years Dizzy Dean was severely criticized for what his drawing-room critics considered a violent abuse of the English language during his broadcasts of baseball. Cultured mothers were horrified and protested. But when he was asked to speak before a forum of his faultfinders he related the misfortune of his childhood which prevented him from "getting hisse'f a eddication." After they had heard his story they were moved with sympathy and exonerated him of the crime with which he was charged.

The duties of these men kept them in the saddle most of the time. There was the roundup in the spring or summer when calves or colts were branded, and when necessary the stock was dipped. In the late summer the salable critters were rounded up and sorted and later driven to the railroads or markets. During the rest of the season they looked after the herds that roamed the range and after the coming of barbwire they rode fence. This is not as severe as the term might indicate. They rode along the miles of wire to mend the breaks and to otherwise keep it in repair. In the winter they were on horseback to look after the welfare of the stock that was out in the open. They braved the biting winds, the stinging sleet and rain and snow to protect and care for the property of their owners and at the close of day they boiled their coffee, baked their biscuits, and fried their bacon at one of the adobe stations set up along the way.

But these weather-beaten sons of the saddle did more than that. They guarded the range against Indian raids and the horse and cattle thieves with which the West was then infested. They were on the outlook for any intruders that threatened the interest of their employer. They were on the watch for rustlers that sometimes made off with large numbers of stock which were driven to distant markets or to other ranges where they were rebranded and incorporated into other herds.

Absence of churches and lack of interest in such affairs were common. And yet they had in them a spark of religion and in some matters they were deeply conscientious. They were superstitious—almost fatalists. They were careless about their use of sacred terminology, and yet they had some conscience even in such matters. The incident is related of a new cow hand whose profanity was so terrible that the rest of the men were afraid to sleep near him on nights when there were thunderstorms. Once on the long trail drive to the railroad one of them became careless, so the story goes, and failed to move his bed when the storm broke. The next morning he was found dead—struck by a bolt of lightning. This made a profound impression upon the outfit. Evidently their consciences were stirred and their superstition deepened. The tragedy is reported to have had a salutary effect upon the language of the entire outfit during the rest of the trip.

On the whole, they were goodhearted people. They were

69

kind, considerate, and helpful. A woman was nowhere more safe than in the care of the simplehearted sons of the open spaces. For recreation they engaged in such pastimes, amusements, and entertainments as they knew, many of which would be considered improper in the circles in which you and I move.

The buckaroo that I knew was not so much attached to an outfit. The cayuses ran loose on the desert range. Some of the men gave most of their time to the work. Others were hired for the roundup and then engaged in other occupations the remainder of the year. There were a few large horse companies in the section where we lived. One was the Gable or otherwise known as the Bracket H outfit. Across the river, the Columbia, was the Benson Ranch which had many horses on the range and some cattle.

The buckaroo was one of the most picturesque characters in the country. His bearing, his swaggering gait, his language, and his equipment set him apart as a class. His outfit consisted of such things as were necessary for him to carry on his work and was neither elaborate nor expensive when compared with the movie or dude ranch cowpunchers of today. Aside from his ordinary clothing it consisted of the following items which were considered essentials. The most prized part of his equipment was his saddle. In my day it would have cost around fifty dollars. Many of the men, however, paid as much as one to two hundred dollars for stamped or hand-tooled ones. A good bridle, a pair of spurs, a wide-brimmed hat, a pair of high-heeled boots, and goat-skin chaps with the hairy side turned out, constituted the major part of his outfit. But the Colt's 45, a cartridge belt, quirt, lariat, and blankets were indispensable and no less important than the horse and saddle.

In the cattle country east of the Rockies, east and central Texas, the saddle was a heavy, double-cinched affair. In the northwest, Oregon, Washington, and in southwest

Texas, it was what is known as three-quarter rigged, which meant a single cinch. California and states adjoining it on the east used what was termed the center fire or half-rigged which was also single cinched. Compared with the modern dude ranch outfit with decorated and tooled chaps, embroidered boots and shirt, and ten-gallon hat, the buckaroos I knew looked rather drab.

There were often serious outbursts of misbehavior, wild celebrations, and many rough times when they came to the towns at the trail's end with their herds. Otherwise they were a dependable set of men. Among them were bad men who seemed to enjoy trouble. They usually did not stay long at a place but while they did they performed their duties well. Since some of them were not in good standing with the law it was the rule among foremen or employers when they hired men not to ask what their real names were. They only wanted to know in what name they wanted their check made out.

The wild life of the West was not confined to the circle of stockmen and their employers. The worst element on the frontier were the gamblers and bad men who found security in the depth of large spaces to which the arm of the law had not reached. They were the killers, bandits, cattle thieves, and outlaws that were responsible for much of the trouble in those quarters. Every community had its quota of these men who continued their depredations until they were wiped out by the officers or the court and legal procedures, when they finally penetrated their field of operation, placed them where they belonged.

It is said that the stockmen reached the country before the law did. Then the primitive code of tooth and claw prevailed. Participants in a quarrel adjudicated their own cases and the verdict was nearly always in favor of the one who was quickest on the draw. With the influx of the lawless and vicious elements some attempt was made to set up

71

tribunals before which cases could be heard. Territorial courts were also established but they were few and far between. The judgeships were often filled by incompetent men who cared more for their own welfare than for that of the community. When conditions became too bad the citizens took matters in hand and organized committees known as the vigilantes. These groups did not consist of the riff-raff of the neighborhood but of the best people. They did not act on impulse but aimed to give the accused a fair hearing and render a just verdict as far as that was possible. In case of guilt the penalty was severe and as swift as it was sure. Many a person dangled from the end of a rope to pay the price for his misdeeds. Committees sprang up in almost every one of the communities and took care of situations that were out of bounds or beyond the control of officers and such courts as existed.

In many places self-styled judges set up in business and later got themselves elected to office. Many of these men were uneducated and had no knowledge of legal matters. Some of them could read only with difficulty. Many of them did good work in keeping order although people often suffered as a result of their unorthodox procedures or unprincipled decisions. This they tolerated because it was largely through the influence of these courts that the lawless were brought under control or eliminated and living in those parts became possible. Some of these men enforced their decisions at the point of their Colt's 45 or Winchesters whenever their word was not adequate to make their rulings effective.

They were for the most part colorful characters. Perhaps none was more so than Roy Bean, "The Law West of the Pecos." Stories about him spread far beyond his jurisdiction and if half of what is said about him is true, it is sufficient to justify the notoriety that he attained. Tradition has it that he was born in Kentucky. His clash with the law it is said brought him before the courts on a number of occasions and made it advisable for him to move frequently from place to place. These migrations took him to Mexico, California, New Mexico, Arizona, and finally to Texas. His experience with the courts furnished him with a smattering of legal terminology and with what little knowledge of judicial procedure he had. When the Southern Pacific was building its tracks through the South Texas country, Roy followed up the railroad and sold what it took to quench the thirst of the hard-drinking Irishmen who constituted the construction crews. His last move was to the place where a town was laid out which the judge called Vinegaroon which he later changed to Langtry.

Here he set himself up as a justice, a position to which he was regularly elected for many years. With such knowledge as he had gleaned through his experience and observations and what little facilities he had for study, he assumed the duties of his office and acted upon such cases as came before his court for adjudication. He not only served as judge but as was frequently the case in those far sections he also acted as coroner. In cases involving the service of the coroner it was, during that time, the policy of having the subjects brought to the office where the inquest was then held. The officer then took charge of the body and all the personal effects of the deceased, made such investigations as were deemed necessary and passed judgment on the affair. One day, so it is said, the body of a man who had come to an untimely demise was delivered to Roy's office. After the inquest was completed he asked: "Jest what did this man do to get hisse'f killed?"

"He was caught stealing, yore honor," was the reply.

"Well, that's agin the law," the judge said, "and for that I'll fine him ten dollars. But since he ain't got but five, I'll hold his gun for security."

By such means it is said that some of these jurists succeeded in building up sizable arsenals, which no doubt stood them in good stead at times when their "rulins" were difficult to enforce.

As the fame of Roy's judicial practices spread, duly elected officers felt that he should give an accounting of the fees he collected and bring his procedures in line with the established order throughout the state. To these demands he replied: "Don't worry none about me. I am aimin' to make my court self-sustainin'!" In this it is said that he succeeded very well. His court not only sustained itself but it was actually in a very flourishing condition financially.

From other sections come stories of the practices of these frontier coroner-jurists, who did what they could to stem the tide of lawlessness and mete out justice to those who had little regard for any interests save their own. It may be said also that some of them were not unmindful of their own interest and along with an attempt to administer justice they looked well after their own affairs. Such as was the case when a hard-working Irishman came to his death in a perfectly honorable and legitimate manner when he accidently fell off a high bridge on the construction of which he was employed. During the inquest the coroner found that the man had a six-shooter in his pocket, together with a roll of bills. Upon this discovery the weapon was confiscated and the corpse was fined an amount that equaled the sum found on his body. There is also the case of a Chinaman who was slain during one of the frontier brawls. The slayer appeared in court accompanied by a formidable gang who proceeded to impress the judge with the eventualities that might follow a wrong decision. During this procedure the justice was earnestly leafing through his "statute book" to find a "precedent or rulin" to help him out of his difficulty. When he finally rapped for order he announced that "the law is explicit on the killing of a fellow man but it says nothing about knocking off a Chinaman." With this the case was dismissed. The "rulin" appeared satisfactory to the boisterous crowd and business at the bar took an immediate upward trend.

Stories such as these seem, no doubt, to many like idle tales drawn from a land of unreality but they are true nevertheless. The absence of an orderly society, and the presence of many who were untutored and lawless made necessary improvised measures which opened the way for legal practices and proceedings which would under other conditions not have been condoned. The men who assumed the role of peace officers and jurists and made themselves responsible for the maintenance of order and to bring the bad element of their day to justice, occupied a tremendously important place in the affairs of their communities. They had their own ideas of how the problems of their time should be solved and did what could be done and what had to be done under the circumstances to suppress the lawless and bring order out of the chaos that existed in those wide sparsely populated, ungoverned places at that time.

It must be said, however, that the Old West did not produce all its bad men. Many—perhaps most of them—came from the East and South where they were wanted by the law and rather than submit to the proceedings of the forces of justice in those parts, they fled to other regions for shelter. The following statement made by an "old-timer" when I stopped at his home in Wyoming is probably not far from the truth. "In the early days," he said, "there was lots of bad men out here but they all came from the East."

Appeals from the decisions of the local courts were not looked upon with favor by some of the presiding judges in those sections where the more primitive methods prevailed. Perhaps it was because they did not know how to carry through such procedures or it may have been because they did not want to subject their "rulins" to the scrutiny of a higher judicial body. When such cases did come before the court the judge often ruled promptly and with firmness. Reports are afloat of instances where attorneys in behalf of their clients, petitioned for a hearing in a higher court upon which the accused was sentenced to a term in jail and the appealing lawyer was fined for contempt of court.

The enforcement of penalties was often difficult because of the lack of suitable places of confinement. Jails or prisons that were adequate to hold the lawless that were within or to withstand the onslaughts of their cohorts on the outside, were lacking. Many a sheriff or other peace officer had no place to keep his prisoners except to chain them to trees or logs or to confine them to dwellings, hotel rooms, or other places that were available. The story is told of an officer who chained his prisoner to the post of the bed in which his wife was sleeping with her newly born baby. Perhaps her dissatisfaction with such an arrangement accounted for the speed with which the city fathers brought into existence a suitable calaboose. Because of the lack of proper quarters for the holding of condemned men the time between the imposition of the sentence and execution of the penalty was brief.

Suitable places for the holding of court sessions were also wanting. In many instances there was no room available except the barroom which was frequently owned and operated by the presiding judge himself, who adjourned the sessions often in order that the thirst of the crowd that attended the trial might not suffer. Law enforcement officers, such as sheriffs, were all too frequently drawn from and elected by the votes of their gang. Many of them had criminal records themselves and may even have been fugitives that were wanted in other parts of the country. Federal officers and the Rangers were important factors in bringing order out of the turbulent situation which existed in many places. They were swift on the draw, dependable and reliable, and as a rule brought in those they were sent for or left them at some outdoor or open-air morgue along the way. Such men as Wyatt Earp, Jeff Milton, Commodore Owen, George Scarborough, and a host of others played important roles in the establishment of order in their day and time.

Gradually as new territories were organized and Federal Courts were established conditions improved. Judges, well trained in their field, were appointed and with their coming more orderly ways and means of handling the problems of the motley population emerged. Judge Parker of Oklahoma and Texas, Judge Grooscup of the Northwest, and others of like ability and incorruptible integrity, by their knowledge and fairness, did much to build up a respect for the law in those parts of the country. By the opening of the twentieth century the Old West was on its way to becoming subdued and brought under control except in some isolated pockets or remote spots where something of the old order remained.

During our sojourn in the West I sat in justice courts and watched the proceedings presided over by officers who knew nothing of the law nor of legal procedures. When driven hard by the opposing attorneys they listened to the evidence and when it was all in, the court was adjourned and the case taken under advisement. Then with the counsel of an attorney, the confused jurist was guided through the maze of legal technicalities and helped to arrive at a decision.

Life in those parts was hard but the seasoned veterans of the ranches and mines had in addition to their courage, self-reliance, and self-sufficiency a sense of humor which enabled them to see the funny side of many of their harsh experiences.

In all the vast, sandy, rough, thinly populated regions, there was perhaps nothing that furnished them with more exciting topics of conversation than did the pack of camels which Jeff Davis had imported from Arabia in 1856 during his tenure as Secretary of State to replace the mules and donkeys as the burden bearers of the desert. This project was not a success, for it was found that these animals did not fit into the American situation. Hence this national experiment, like many others since that day, was a total loss, unless the excitement and humor which these long-necked quadrupeds contributed to the life of their time can be considered an asset.

When this venture became recognized as a failure the camels were turned loose and eventually became scattered over wide areas covering parts of several states and furnished the meager population with weird and exciting tales to enliven the drabness of its lonely life. A young lad came in one day and declared he had seen an antelope with a neck like a goose.

Perhaps none of these episodes, so loaded with near tragedy and humor, was more widely known than that which took place when one day a young Mexican lassoed one of these queer-looking ruminants and brought it into one of the frontier towns where he succeeded in getting one of his creditors to accept it in payment of a small debt. After the deal was completed he rode away leaving the animal tied to the hitching rack in front of what was known was the Bon Ton Saloon.

A crowd soon collected. When the details of the transaction became known the new owner became the victim of all the jibes and wit his fellow townsmen could think of. They evidently needed some release of the tensions under which they labored so much of the time during those days.

While the poor beast was standing in the midst of the hilarious gathering, a citizen of the town in a fit of humor "goosed" it with the end of his cane. This touched off a series of events that for several days threatened to turn the town into a shambles and precipitated a fracas that it took some time to undo.

Not accustomed to the crude American pranks the animal reared back into a buggy, flattened a wheel or so on the off side, and sent a frantic team of horses galloping down the road with a vehicle bouncing at its heels. In its anxiety to get away from the rude jesting crowd it tore loose the hitching rail to which it had been tethered which then swung at the end of the rope like an I-beam at the end of a crane and went down the dusty thoroughfare smashing right and left while the gleeful citizens scampered hither and yon to escape the dangling pole and the bewildered beast.

As a result of this funny streak of one of its townsmen, the Bon Ton suffered the loss of its porch roof when the props were knocked out from under it. The watering trough was upset early in the scramble. The water cooler at the saloon was broken, the sidewalk furniture wrecked, windows and plate-glass fronts smashed. One of the citizens was laid low when the long pole gave him a bump on the head and the owner of the frightened quadruped got mixed up with the rope and escaped with a burn on the side of his neck and his ear dangling by the lobe. This first act of the drama came to a close when the beast was captured in some lady's flower bed. The owner then sought out the "goosing" prankster and demanded that he share the cost of pacifying the community for damages of this upheaval.

But the end was not yet. When a few days later a young Indian agreed to take the animal out to the far side of the desert the owner felt relieved. But instead this was the beginning of the second act. En route out of town a team went "loco" when it saw the form of the strange, odorous beast and upset a load of hay into an irrigation ditch. This blocked the stream and caused the ditch to overflow. It then flooded an alfalfa field, "melted" the dirt foundation of an adobe dwelling, which collapsed, drowned the chickens and stirred up feelings in the bosom of the owner that weren't good.

79

Some days later, the owner of the camel, with his ear stitched back in place, armed with a high-caliber rifle, took his much-berated animal far out beyond the bounds of human habitation where he intended to put an end to its career. But when he saw the bewildered, solitary figure, standing confused like in its desolate surroundings, something fine on the inside of him was touched. After thinking things over he "allowed that it wa'nt the pore beast's fault. It was a stranger in the land and it was those fool men that caused the trouble," he mused. He "figgered" that it ought to have a chance to live. So he turned it loose and left it to its fate, far from its Arabian home and its kith and kin, among a queer people whose ways and manners it never learned to understand or appreciate.

The flaming days of the Old West are gone but the bad men and lurid women are still with us. Today they do not find their most fruitful fields of operation nor their retreats and hide-outs along the towns and resorts of the far-flung open plains or desert but in the congested metropolitan centers where the masses congregate. The fields of their activities have shifted now but the spirit of those that live and work outside of the law is no less harsh or cruel or merciless than it was during the hard days of the Old Frontier and, besides, the chivalry that marked it then is lacking now.

Civilization, culture, and education are no certain cure for the vices and evils of our day any more than they were of other days. These factors often make it possible for crime to operate under a respectable guise and in a decent setting, but it is still sin and crime as it always was since the race began.

If the agencies upon which the world has depended for its development and security have failed, where then may we look for relief? Peace officers, jurists, and others who are charged with the responsibility of maintaining order and decency are deeply concerned with what is happening around us. In many instances these officers find themselves greatly handicapped with the manner in which a large number of what passes as respectable citizens look upon violations of the law and the moral let-down all over the land. It is easy as well as popular to lay the blame upon the doorstep of Communism or upon the shoulders of law-enforcing agencies, or legislators who are more concerned with the security of their position than they are in enacting legislation that will curb the evil and promote the good. Or we accuse the liquor interests, movies, and other recreational activities which have been captured by commercial organizations who operate them for their own gain regardless of what happens to the morals, the character, and life of those who come under their influence.

No doubt there is all too much truth in the above charges but there are many reformers, educators, Christian ministers, laymen, social workers, and peace officers who believe that even though all the above-mentioned factors could be wiped out we would still have the problem with us. They believe that the root of evil resides in the unregenerate human heart—or call it nature if you will. They believe, too, that the remedy lies in a deep and abiding faith in God as a person to whom all will be held accountable for what they do. He, the God of Abraham, has given us a code of morals at Sinai that is irrevocably in harmony with His will, and Christ set forth principles of life and character that will lift man out of the morass of sin.

We condemn the modern social agencies for the moral delinquencies of our youth. But one wonders whether the home has not shifted too much of its responsibility to the multiplicity of organizations spawned and set up by the church, but which too many have accepted as a means whereby they may be relieved of their own obligations.

81

The mountains have put on
Their robes of midnight blue
And settled down to sleep
Beneath the sky.
The moon in gold beret
Is coyly peeping through
The shirred and ruffled clouds
As they drift by.
The cowled and cossacked palms
Like cloistered monks in line
Recite nocturnal Mass
With rustling breeze
And droning insect choirs,
Before a hidden shrine,
Religiously intone
Responsories.

Margaret Wheeler Rose

VII

A Day with the Roundup

Ting-a-ling, a-ling, a-ling came the sound of the bells on the saddle herd, one hundred and fifty strong, followed by the night herders. They were rounding the hill at the mouth of the large coulee near the camp when the first rays of the coming daylight made their appearance in the east.

The night had seemed very short and the weary bodies of the men, tired from the long ride of the previous day, were not nearly rested. The outfit had moved camp and picked up what horses it could get along the way. When the men in charge of the rodeo reached the corrals they had more than a thousand head besides the remuda which had reached the place long before the main body. The drive had led along the foot of the mountains, a very rough and hilly country. It was a hard one to ride because of the rocks and hills and coulees to which these hill horses retreated as soon as they saw the dust rising out of the tracks of the oncoming herd. When they reached the river they turned southward and followed its course to Muir's Landing where they corraled for the next few days while they were riding that part of the range.

The remuda furnished mounts for the twenty-five or more buckaroos who changed horses every day. It was taken out by the night herders to graze on the open country which furnished the only feed available. While on the roundup the men lived off the chuck wagon but the work animals had to live off the country.

When awakened by the bells of the incoming saddle herd, the men turned over in their bed rolls and had just dozed off to sleep again, when the cook gleefully—so it seemed— began to beat time on the huge triangle which hung on the corner of the chuck wagon, informing them that breakfast was ready. There was nothing for an honorable buckaroo to do but to crawl out, roll up his bedding, toss it under the wagon, and get ready for another day's ride.

By the time they had washed in the cool waters of the river they were thoroughly awake, and their stiffened joints had become sufficiently limbered up for the day. Then they hastened to the chuck wagon for their cups of coffee and plates of bacon and beans and biscuits. After breakfast each one made for the corral to select his mount. After considerable confusion, whirring of lariats, and a frequent abuse of polite language, they were ready for the drive.

While rounding up in this section the horses were pastured on the island at night but in daytime they had to be loose-herded on the range. To gather up one thousand of these wild, untamed creatures and swim them across the channel each morning was a thrilling experience. As soon as they had been turned loose each stallion gathered his band around himself. They were alert and wary. The years had made them wise and at the first sight of a man mounted on horseback they were off. Over toward the far end of the island, which was more than a mile long and two thirds that wide, one of these leaders—a beautiful creature—true to his instinct, had taken his position on a little knoll. As soon as the first horseman appeared he gave a shrill snort, at which his band gathered around him and made a dash for freedom. He, however, did not get far, until he saw the uselessness of flight. Then dejected and meek he fell in with the rest of the herd, which was driven to the north end where the channel was narrowest and where the water was shallow enough to be forded or where the horses could easily swim across. To see a thousand wild, struggling cayuses wading, plunging, or swimming through the current was a beautiful sight. Mothers with little colts huddling close to their sides, and horses of all ages, colors, and sizes splashing and dashing for the shore, no doubt with a hope of freedom, was a spectacle one will not soon forget.

All went well, except that Tony, who was a racial mixture of some sort, in order to keep himself from getting wet, had somehow managed to get into a boat with someone to do the rowing for him. He threw the bridle rein carelessly over the pommel of his saddle and turned his mount, a beautiful animal, loose. This faithful creature followed the herd of his own accord and helped to keep it together until he floundered into deep water. In the struggle to get his bearings he got his feet tangled in the reins and before anyone could have come to his rescue he was drowned. Tony felt badly about it—he should have! Why he was accepted by the roundup in the first place is more than I know. He always had what he spoke of as bad luck, which everyone knew was due to negligence and carelessness, often sheer laziness and shiftlessness. There are many like him, who neglect their duty or do their work halfheartedly and thoughtlessly and when evil consequences follow they blame the world for not giving them a fair deal. He was one of them!

After the horses were delivered to the herders the rest of

the men were taken out over the range that was to be covered that day, and were scattered along the route over a distance of many miles. Then they rode toward a given point, driving the loose bands before them from every direction. As they closed in from all sides those that were caught within this net were taken to the corral. There they were looked over and if any were thought salable, or were needed by those whose brand they bore, they were thrown in with the main herd and held. Mares were held until their colts were branded—the colt always took the mother's brand. Then they were turned loose for another year and were soon seen on their range again.

However, not all the horses with the net thrown around them were caught. Many of them dashed by through the gaps between the riders and made their way to freedom. Some did that successfully for years under the guidance of their leader whose instinct invariably served him right. Every range had several bands like that. They were spotted by the men who rode and when one of them was finally captured, the person whose genius and wit enabled him to bring them in was the hero of the outfit.

When the day's drive was over, which was usually about the middle of the afternoon, the men gathered about the chuck wagon where they ate their potatoes and biscuits and bacon and beans. Sometimes there were extras ·such as "Mormon Dip" or "Spotted Pup," depending on how much the cook's soda biscuit dyspepsia was "ailin' him." If it was bad, there were just the bare essentials which were always good and sufficient. On his better days, there was the "Mormon Dip"—gravy made of flour and bacon drippings which was roasted in a skillet and stirred up with water or milk— more often water which the men said was fried until it was brown! This concoction also took the place of butter. What relation that mixture has to do with the Mormons is beyond me. It evidently antedated the history of the boys who rode in the Great Basin in my time, for none of them could "fig-ger" it out either. "Spotted Pup" was not so difficult. It consisted of cooked rice with raisins and was one of the luxuries of the camp, and always assured the cook of some nice compliments spoken in the crude language of these children of the lonely places.

The cooking facilities were primitive and obsolete. Clean-liness may not always have been possible; in fact, it seldom was. "Some ashes and a little dust an' sand don't hurt the food none," they said. Yet these chefs who followed the roundup were experts, and no artist in all the eating places across the world where I have eaten cooked better beans or baked better biscuits—"They're lighter'n hen feathers," they said—than did these simplehearted sons of the plains who cooked and baked by sagebrush fires.

What was left of the day after the ride was over belonged to the men. It was theirs to use as they wished and the time was usually spent in leisure. Horses were looked over; per-haps there was some trading done. Experiences were re-counted and stories were told. Some engaged in games and other amusements. There may have been some melodious buckaroo in the outfit who entertained the rodeo by singing the songs of the desert and the plains. He may even have had a tinny guitar among his belongings.

In the evening the low setting sun brought in the herd which was again placed on the island. The bells of the remuda came tinkling up the coulee and the day men turned it over to the night herders. Then the fires burned low and the voices died down as everyone sought the comfort of his blankets for rest and sleep—all except the cook, who was busy getting things in order for the morning meal. The deep quietness of the summer night was broken only by an occasional splash of water or the doleful howl of some wandering coyote whose notes fell like music upon the ear of a western man and lulled him off to slumberland.

Hast thou given the horse strength?
Hast thou clothed his neck with thunder?
Canst thou make him afraid as a grasshopper?
The glory of his nostrils is terrible.
He paweth in the valley, and rejoiceth in his strength.

Job 39:19-21.

VIII

Riding an Outlaw

Brown lived over by the river in a deserted homestead shack. From somewhere he had accumulated sufficient posts and wire to fence in some land which served as a temporary pasture. He seemed to have come from nowhere when he first appeared on the range and had the very disconcerting habit of riding up to the corrals when horses were being rounded up at off seasons of the year and taking his position on the top railing from which he could see what was going on. Later, it was learned that he came from

89

Texas. One evening after he had filled himself at our table his guard went down and he began to talk. He was a Texas orphan, the child of a stockman. There were no questions asked about his parents. They lived and died at a time when going in Texas was rough. Ever since he was old enough to sit in the saddle he had followed the roundup and the cattle drives across Texas into Oklahoma or New Mexico to the shipping points along the railroad. Nobody knew why he was here but all the owners of range horses had him connected with the Bracket H outfit, although this was never confirmed. He was a lone wolf, as the saying goes, and was liable to show up anywhere. People who had a shady record of handling range stock were never easy or comfortable when he was around.

He came into our little world one Sunday when I saw smoke coming from the flue of a desert shack and rode over to see what was going on. He had evidently tried to prepare something to eat. When I first saw him he was sitting on the sill of a stable while his horse was being fed. Upon my invitation he followed me over to our place where he was given his dinner which he greatly enjoyed and appreciated. After that he stopped with us frequently. He, however, would never consent to sleep inside. He preferred the open spaces as though he did not want to provide an occasion for being cornered.

He was a typical child of the out-of-doors. Experience taught him the necessity of being practical; consequently he had long ago laid aside all the trappings and finery so prized by men of his kind and had replaced his goatskin chaps with ordinary trousers which could at that time have been bought anywhere for three dollars a pair. A broad-brimmed sombrero, silk neck scarf, silver mounted spurs, and high-heeled boots completed his riding outfit. Sometimes he wore his chaps.

After having accompanied him on several short trips for

horses, I found him an expert with the lariat and his several feats of roping I saw on the open range were marvelous. He had an uncanny way with stock and more than once he corraled, singlehandedly and alone, a whole herd of wild horses—outlaw bands! While living at the river he had accumulated a considerable number of Bracket H horses and was holding them for the owner.

On the range there were three bands which successfully eluded the roundup each year, the Dirty Seven's, the Sheddy Eight's, and the Wild Gooses. Each one was under the leadership of a stallion—every band is. Each herd was unbranded which meant that they had never been corraled. They were wild and free as the wind. No hand had ever touched them. They were magnificent in their glory— shrewd, alert, and wary. They had never been conquered. They belonged to anyone who could get them into a corral and stick his brand on them.

One morning when I approached Brown's quarters I saw his gaunt form standing in the doorway of his cabin. His pinched, weather-beaten face beamed as he greeted me and almost shouted as he spoke, "Where do you think the Wild Gooses are?" They were a band of fifteen led by a black stallion who was the coveted prize of the range.

"I don't know," I replied, "unless they are in your pasture," little thinking that such was actually the case.

"That's jest where they are," he proclaimed, "and if you'll lend me a hand I'll ride 'im today," referring, of course, to the leader of the band.

That was just what I wanted to see. I had seen Brown ride bad ones before and he had never failed to stick. But here was a horse, full-grown and mature, that had been the leader of an outlaw band for over five years. No rope had ever fallen over his neck, no saddle had ever graced his back, and no human hand had ever touched his body. He had grown up in freedom, unbridled and unrestrained. He had roamed the range at will since the day he was born and I was anxious to see the outcome of this venture.

We walked out to the pasture, leading our horses till we got up to the herd. Then we mounted quickly, and drove them together into a body so that they would be more easily controlled in case they should start to run. Brown was mounted on Roany, his favorite horse—a tall strawberry roan—and kept circling around them, lariat in hand, waiting for a throw. The shrewd black fellow kept out of his reach, all the while working his way out toward the edge, ready to break away if the opportunity should present itself. Suddenly he made a dash, but Brown was ready for him! A touch of spurs sent Roany after him. Brown gave the rope a whirl and landed it on the outlaw's neck.

Then the scramble began! At one end of the lariat was a wild creature that knew nothing but freedom; at the other end was an experienced roping-horse that was on to all the tricks of his profession. He was fully able to take care of himself as well as the animal at the other end of the rope. The outlaw's wind was soon cut off and he went down. It was an easy matter then to sit on his head and hold him while Brown fastened the saddle, adjusted the hackamore, and got himself into a position to go.

Finally he announced that all was ready. He stood astride the horse with one foot in the stirrup. With one hand he clung to the saddle horn and with the other one he held the end of the hackamore. At a signal from him I let the horse go. As soon as he was released he sprang to his feet. Brown righted himself in the saddle. For a moment the animal stood bewildered, then he gave a snort and the show was on! From the very start it was a guess as to who would win. Brown was an old-timer and had lots of experience with bucking horses. His mount was not an experienced bucker like Midnight and others of their kind who had learned all the tricks of unseating their riders. He kicked and pitched and reared. He did everything he knew to do, but the old buckaroo sat securely. When pitching failed to dislodge his rider, he started to run. When that failed he began to pitch again. He went up and down stiff-legged, with his head between his front legs. He changed ends and reared. Finally he gathered up all his strength, pulled his magnificent body into a knot, as it were, and made one great leap. Then the cinch broke! Brown, clinging to the saddle, rose against the sky line like a balloon. Before he came down the horse was out from under him, and he landed in a bed of prickly pears. Somewhere at the very outset he lost his hat; his three-dollar trousers were hopelessly wrecked; his leg was full of cactus thorns, but his temper was unruffled. No man could have treated this Texan that way and lived, but a wild horse could!

"Say," he said, as he scrambled to his feet, "them there stickers on them prickly pears is 'bout as long as a porka-pine's quills."

He began to pull the cactus thorns out of his leg and every time he got one, he paused and gazed after the Wild Gooses that had cleared the fence and were fleeing toward the Sad-dle Mountains over to the north.

But the spell of the outlaw's charmed life was broken. The confidence with which he led his band was gone. Some months later Brown came upon this outfit again and had them between the wagon trail that led across the country from the river to the railroad and the fence of his pasture. By skillful maneuvering he succeeded in getting them inside the fence. This time he held on to the black stallion and soon had him under control and made him an honorable and worthy member of his saddle herd, which was among the best in the country.

Give ear, O ye heavens, and I will speak;
And hear, O earth, the words of my mouth.
My doctrine shall drop as the rain,
My speech shall distil as the dew,
As the small rain upon the tender herb,
And as the showers upon the grass:
Because I will publish the name of the Lord:
Ascribe ye greatness unto our God.

Deuteronomy 32:1-3

IX

Rain in the Desert

It's raining in the desert today! Last night the stars that usually twinkle like unnumbered jewels in a vault of blue shone sickly as they do in other lands of murky skies. Moisture gathered into clouds along the mountainsides and floated out across the valleys until all the nightly hosts were shut out. Then the rain came! A quiet, soothing rain that distilled as the dew and came "as the small rain upon the tender herb, and as the showers upon the grass." A rain which the poet said:

> . . . is murmuring as if in prayer,
> Telling of wonders born of sky and air.

For months the sky had been barren—it was late in August. The sun had been pouring its barbs of heat down through an ashen sky till the earth seemed lifeless and burned out. The sparse vegetation that sprang forth in response to the scanty precipitation of the previous winter and spring was gone. Flowers dried up and were carried away by the winds. The sagebrush curled up its little gray leaves, closed its pores, and settled down to a life and death struggle with the wind and weather. Cattle lingered by the springs at noontide and bands of wild horses made long excursions to the back side of the desert in search of food. Wild life gathered in the shadow of the great rocks and buttes and behind coulee walls to escape the heat of the sun and the sweep of the hot winds.

Then it rained one Sunday morning during our sojourn in the desert, after long months of dewless nights and hot wind-blown days. How good the earth smelled when the first drops touched the toasted soil and how the sage unfurled its leaves and from its open pores poured forth an aroma like incense from an altar of God!

The casual stranger who ventures within the gates of this wide, dried out area that stretches on and on for seemingly countless miles during the rainless period sees only the immensity of the vast waste and barrenness whose solitude fairly shriek's against such intrusion. To him it seems unfriendly, foreboding—even frightening. And well it may, for the bleaching bones of those who perished beside its trails bear ample testimony to its harsher moods. But it isn't always thus. Its bedraggled and forlorn appearance needs some defense at the forum of inexperienced opinion that sees nothing but waste and emptiness in this wide expanse. To its friends and acquaintances, however, it is kind. How it coaxes and lures me to linger on every time I step within its borders! And how I am tempted to forego my responsibilities and stay in its restful atmosphere! Its quietness brings new vigor and hope to jaded spirits that smother and suffocate in the jostling crowds where human unkindness lurks and lives. Its wide stretching spaces make room for the soul's expansion and amid its solitude great thoughts are born. Did not Jesus turn to such wilds to prepare His soul for the crisis of the temptation, and was not John the Baptist a child of the desert, a brother to the hot winds, to cloudless days and starry nights? Such was the region to which Elijah fled in the days of his trouble with Jezebel, and here is where Amos gathered the thunder for the message which he hurled so passionately at Israel in the markets of Samaria. Abraham gazed into the desert night out of Babylonia and Syria. Isaac and Jacob pastured their herds on the scanty grasses of the Mesopotamian and Palestinian plains. Moses grazed his flocks on the desert of Midian. Great names and great souls these are—they lived in the plains under barren skies, these men whose names are secure in the gallery of the Immortals.

And what records the desert has made in history! Recent excavations in Babylonia and Assyria, watered only by the courses of the Euphrates and the Tigris, astound the modern world with the grandeur and excellence of their culture, their literature and science and art. Research among the ancient ash heaps and dumping grounds of Egypt reveals a civilization that was hoary with age when first the dawn of history broke. What wonders the ancient Incas wrought on the barren hillsides and plains of Peru and the Mound Builders and their predecessors in New Mexico and our own Southwest!

Therefore, speak softly when you talk disparagingly of these seemingly worthless wastes, for the voices that cry from these ancient mounds will confuse and confound you and nations will rise from the dust into which they have fallen, to witness against your testimony. Thebes and Memphis, and Damascus and Nineveh and Babylon, and all the towns of ancient lore will not keep silent in the face of erroneous representation. Here in these unwatered areas

is found much of the world's choicest treasures of the mine—
her gold and silver and copper. In her bosom are rivers of
oil, and the soil of her hills and valleys, when touched by
the waters of friendly streams, directed by the mind of those
who love and understand its whims and whiles and changing
moods, springs forth into life and blossoms as the rose.

And then what noble use the writers of Scripture have
made of its forms and features. When looking about for
adequate figures to describe the Hope of Israel, Isaiah drew
on the desert for some of his choicest types and allusions—

> For he shall grow up before him
> As a tender plant,
> And as a root out of a dry ground;
> He hath no form nor comeliness;
> And when we shall see him,
> There is no beauty that we should desire him.
>
> *Isaiah 53:2*

Or the psalmist who sings of the excellence of the name
of the Lord in all the earth, who has set His glory above
the heavens! He pictures the righteous as a tree planted by
rivers of water, that brings forth his fruit in his season, and
the wicked as the chaff which the wind sweeps away.

The Book of Joel, with its drought and insect plague, with
its lowing flocks and starving herds, presents a scene that
was laid on the fringe of the desert. From Genesis to Reve-
lation all writers, poets, priests, and prophets have found in
its climatology, its earth forms, its life, its wild moods, its
idiosyncrasies, illustrations that were adequate for their
need and in its language they expressed the great truths of
God! The Scripture teems with these types and figures.

The desert has not outlived its usefulness. These are days
when people are tremendously hard on each other and the
worn and tired spirits of humankind need rest. They seek
it at the watering places and other resorts where the crowds

collect; where sin broods over the multitude and evil thoughts are born—in these nests of vice and pleasure. Or they look for it on the highways where danger lurks, where the fumes of gasoline drown the fragrance of the soil and blooming flowers, and the noise of passers-by obscures the song of the birds and the rustling of the leaves.

The stress and strain of our daily lives requires rest. Human greed and unkindness and selfishness, that all too often pollute the atmosphere of the ordinary life, make necessary retirement to the retreats which the All-wise Maker so abundantly provided in the wide reaches of the desert and plains and in the hills of God. Here in quietness and confidence the soul may find new strength, and here the mind is never wearied with the cares and distractions of modern life. People may look for this lordly heritage where they will, but some of us, who have learned to love the barren expanses, seek for peace in these quiet places. Having learned to know them we go back again and again only to come away with renewed vigor, refreshed in mind and body and spirit and with a more healthy outlook on life and its problems.

Keep silence, and open wide your soul!—it's raining in the desert today.

No, I am not afraid to face
The vast deep sweep of endless space
When far into the heart of the wild I am drawn,
Where the gray line of the purple sage
Marks the place of the dawn.

X

Riding for Rustlers

For years the horsemen of Columbia Flat had suffered at the hands of rustlers which was only a polite name for horse thieves. Perhaps none of them were more affected by these predatory bands than was Henry Gable, proprietor of the Bracket H outfit. When he was young and could withstand the rigors of the range he prospered. But now that the years hung heavily upon him he didn't ride much and had to depend upon hired help to look after his stock. Since his horses were the best bred of any on the range they were coveted by others and he was much imposed on. Some of the men who worked for him even may have played into the hands of those whose conscience was not too keen in the matter of getting the proper brand on the Gable colts.

Early in the spring when the horses were yet weak from the ravages of winter some of those who had brands on this range—and some who did not—would sweep across the country and gather up what animals they could get, drive them to some isolated corral, cut out those that were considered unsafe to take, and make good their escape with the rest.

This particular winter had been unusually severe and stock came out of it very thin. Brown, who lived on the range, and knew all the ways of the wild, had been noticing that the horses were much disturbed lately and suspected that some of these early rounders were at work. When a horseman appeared the scattered bands were off for the security of the coulees or their mountain retreats from which it was difficult to dislodge them. Of course at this season, early spring, they were always more or less restless, but now they were much on the move and appeared to be much disturbed. Naturally a person thought of rustlers although none had thus far been seen.

One evening about dusk Brown rode up to our corral with the information that he had been following a band for several days. They had gathered up one hundred or more head by this time, he judged. His conclusion was that they had come from the upper country which meant from the North. They had stayed along the foot of the Saddle Mountains within the shelter of the foothills and coulees, he observed. Tonight, he opined, they were headed for the corral at the Bluffs and tomorrow, he thought, they would make their way to Waluke where they would cut out what they didn't want and get out of the country as rapidly as possible.

Brown insisted that this outfit had to be followed and if it turned out to be what he suspected it had to be broken up. "They are don goin' to be rough," he said, "but we cain't let them git out of the country with them there hosses." I agreed with what he said—"They are don goin' to be rough." He concluded correctly that it was too late to get help from Scootney, Gable's headquarters, and urged that

102

someone from our place go along with him. "Take along your Winchester and whatever hardware you have," he insisted.

Brown did not have too many friends in these parts. Many of the stockmen were suspicious of him, perhaps because their hands weren't as clean as they should have been. It did not take much persuasion, although I realized the possibility of what all might happen, but I was young and curious and was eager to see what could be done by way of putting an end to this nefarious business. Everybody with range stock had suffered at the hands of these prowlers and it was time to break up the gang and put a stop to their dishonorable and illegitimate operations.

That night he slept out by a pile of hay as usual, but we were out early. The morning was crisp—sharply cold. A white frost covered the ground. After riding a while we dismounted, built a sagebrush fire, and toasted our toes till we were thoroughly warmed up. Before we got to the river we saw something we could hardly believe. We crossed the tracks of the herd going east! Instead of going north to Waluke as we had supposed, they had turned and were backtracking. They had beat us to the trail and were no doubt on the way out. They evidently had started before dawn, for they were already out of sight. The trampled turf showed that they were taking a northeasterly course. Brown was an old-timer, rich with experience in matters of this kind. He concluded that they would follow the foot of the mountain to what was known as the point of the hill where the Saddle Mountains ran out and melted into the plain, as the saying was. There, he thought, they would turn north and corral for the night at Crab Creek, or perhaps at Moses Lake, although the latter was not likely on account of the distance. They would then do what he had expected them to do at Waluke—cut out the undesirable stock and make off with the rest.

103

At his suggestion we decided it unnecessary to follow them around the hill, but thought it best to cross the mountain and be at the corral to meet them when they came in with the herd. We left the trail and leisurely ascended the slope to a homesteader's cabin where we found a supply of canned goods and some crackers. In accordance with the custom of the country we exercised our right and made a meal of cold tomatoes, pork and beans, and crackers. I never knew before that food out of tin cans was so good!

Sometime before midafternoon we reached the barren summit and unwisely stopped to scan the plain below for a glimpse of the outfit. All at once we saw a streak of dust rising out of a gully at the foot of the hills not far from where we sat and suddenly there burst out of the coulee a band of mountain horses followed by several men. We watched them going through the brush and farther on we saw the large band through the haze of dust which hung concealingly over the gray sage that covered the country. Then we saw the men on horseback fan out and open the north side of the main herd to make way for these newcomers to enter. The trick was so neatly done that we were sure the outfit was made up of old hands who understood their business.

With a feeling of certainty that we had correctly interpreted the intentions of the gang, and relieved of the responsibility of trailing it through the brush and dust, we had time to enjoy our surroundings of which the plainsman never tires. While resting on a knoll on the steeply descending side of the Saddle Mountains we saw in the spreading valley below a band of horses grazing peacefully and contentedly as range horses do. Suddenly the breeze must have carried to them the scent of sweaty leather even though they were far off. The leader became very restless. He took his place on a little raise. With his wild head erect and with his mane ruffled by the wind he scanned the country around him. Then he charged around his band, drove them together, and returned to his observation point where with every nerve tense he again looked for the encroaching danger, apparently giving warning to his herd with shrill snorts from his widely dilated nostrils. We watched him going through his performances for some time before he saw us. Finally he discovered the source of their possible trouble. With the precision of one who is in command he took his place at the head of his little group and dashed away into a coulee where they disappeared—all except the dust they raised.

During what remained of that afternoon I also saw one of the prettiest feats of outside roping I had ever witnessed. We came upon a band of some twelve or fifteen horses which we succeeded in getting under control when they suddenly came up against a wire fence. Among them was a Bracket H saddle horse that had gotten away and joined these wild ones. We held them until Brown got his lariat ready. Then he ordered, "Let 'em go," which I did. Long-legged, fleet-footed Roany—what a horse he was!—seemed thrilled with the prospect and immediately sensed which animal was wanted. A flap of his master's chaps against the saddle sent him off while the rope whined through the air and fell over the head of the prodigal that had left his chief's corral and board. He was snubbed to the saddle horn and led to a pasture into which he was turned until a more convenient time when he was restored to the saddle herd at Scootney.

Later in the day we arrived at the cabin and corrals on the creek. We found the man who lived close by very uncommunicative and inhospitable. He even declined to give us our supper and was not happy about letting us sleep on the remnants of what was once a haystack. This made us all the more certain that we were on the right track because we believed that he was no doubt a "stool pigeon" which these rustlers had posted to set off the alarm and alert them of danger. No doubt he knew of their plans and was not pleased with our presence. He wanted no loose horsemen or wandering scouts in the neighborhood when they brought in the horses for the night. Brown's connection with the Gable outfit followed him like Hamlet's ghost wherever he went from the North Country to the Snake River. He told me one time, "These buckaroos don't love me non, 'cause they cain't make me out." That was true. Those who handled brands carelessly and by shady methods were in danger all the time. No one knew when this solitary figure would come riding ghostlike out of the brush and catch them red-handed in trouble-laden business.

We rode up the creek to a vacant cabin which contained some evidences of being occupied but the occupants were gone. Here we found feed for our horses, ate what we could find, and gathered up some hay and straw for a bed. The hard day's ride, and the unfriendliness of the man at the corral were discouraging and disturbing. It didn't make us feel good. We waited and waited for the noise of the trampling hoofs of the incoming herd. Our nerves were tense—at least mine were! Every sound in the darkness took on a meaning. Every sigh of the wind, every plunge of bullfrogs into the water, the buzzing wings of the nighthawk or the footfalls of roaming stock were grasped at intently as evidence of their coming. But we waited in vain.

Brown unbuckled his belt and laid his unholstered Colt's where it was handy to get. Upon seeing my evident lack of regard for what he considered a necessary precaution for the emergency which might suddenly arise, he advised: "You all better lay that there hardware of yourn where hit's haindy. I ain't skittish none but I ain't aimin' to take no chainces." So that was it! He was really expecting that there might be bad trouble. I knew that these fellows would be rough if we caught up with them if they were who and what Brown thought they were. He actually expected that

106

this business might become serious. Here in this spot the spirit of the Old West remained!

We were finally tucked into the hay and covered with our blankets. Our saddles sheltered our heads against the night breeze which was blowing stiffly. The cold moon rose out of the east and sailed calmly along the crest of the Saddle Mountains. Finally we dropped off into a disturbed slumber. Once when I was awake during the early part of the night I heard the footfalls of a lone horse going through the sage-brush—perhaps that's what awakened me. It was not the slow, irregular tread of one that was grazing along, but the regular hoofbeat of a horse that is under the saddle. Maybe it was a messenger sent by our inhospitable friend on his way to warn the rustlers of danger. Who knows?

When we woke the next morning the sun was peeping over the hills and a new day had dawned. We rode over to the corrals and found them empty. No horseman had appeared. We rode back to our grumpy friend of the night before and found him in a better mood. The restlessness which was so evident during our previous meeting was gone. He seemed relieved—perhaps because the herd didn't show up. At any rate this man who was so unfriendly and discourteous the day before now invited us into his cabin for a breakfast of pancakes, soda biscuits, ham and eggs, which his wife had prepared. She was hospitable and kind. There was no evidence of apprehension about her and her attitude was almost apologetic. I presume she tried to atone for her husband's rudeness of the previous evening. At any rate she gave us a good breakfast. When we rode away we agreed that she probably did not approve of his conduct. Perhaps she did not even suspect the cause as we did.

We retraced our steps and at the point of the hill we picked up the trail and saw that for some reason the outfit suddenly turned south instead of north as we had anticipated. Later we learned that evidence had been secured from residents scattered throughout the country which was sufficient to identify some of the parties and bring them to justice.

Late in the afternoon, long hours after breakfast at Crab Creek, we rode up to a cabin hoping to find something that would make us a meal. All we discovered was a small piece of bacon and a little bag of sugar. This afforded us the wherewithal for our supper. There was no dietitian present to inform us of the nutritive deficiency of such a diet and since we knew nothing of calories and vitamins we suffered no evil consequences. Late in the night I rode up to our corrals. Hours before, no doubt, Brown had rolled in his blankets on the rim of the extinct volcanic crater at Scootney, the headquarters of the Gable outfit.

We were safely home. The rustlers were at least scared out of their earlier plans and were headed for justice. A Bracket H horse had been salvaged and was securely pastured where at a more convenient time he could be picked up and replaced in the remuda. On the whole the trip was considered a success.

Picking up horses off the range looked easy at that time and many who undertook it got by. But people cannot permanently escape the consequences of their misdeeds. Sooner or later sin catches up with its deluded victims and they are forced to pay the price which the laws of justice irrevocably demand. The age-old proverb and saying of the Scripture: "The way of the transgressor is hard," and "He that soweth to the wind shall reap the whirlwind" is still true. Long years of experience and observation make me more sure than ever that it does not pay to tamper with the great, eternal principles of righteousness. This was true of the horse thieves who operated in the limitless expanses where the population was sparse and the conventional ways of meting out justice were weak. It is also true of the misdemeanors which are so common in our own day and time.

On the whole those who had horses on the range were honorable and trustworthy men. There were, however, those who took advantage of situations to add to their own herds by means which were not at all conventional. There were those too, who contributed to the grief of the stockmen of this area. They were the nesters—those who settled on the land with the hope of turning it into farms or wheatlands. Some of them took an unwholesome attitude toward stock which caused problems and losses among stockmen. Among these settlers there were also those who could not resist the temptation of gathering up a few head here and there and driving them off to distant markets to replenish their failing financial resources. Such unorthodox acts by these novices of the plains soon came to grief and ended disasterously which afforded them the opportunity of reflecting on their misdeeds behind quieting and secure walls of stone and bars of steel.

. . . . Take the wings
Of morning, pierce the Barcan wilderness,
Or lose thyself in the continuous woods
Where rolls the Oregon, and hears no sound
Save his own dashing. . . .

William Cullen Bryant

XI

A Runaway on the Columbia

The only way by which the Columbia River can be crossed after it tumbles down over the rocks at Priest Rapids and finds its composure again in its widened channel, is by ferry. Some of these flat, squatty contrivances were in our day pushed back and forth across the stream by little gas engines. They were mounted outside of the railings which enclosed the boat and served as corrals for stock and sideboards for freight. These little motors take their work seriously and chug and rattle and bang as they transport their cargo from one side of the river to the other. When they do not receive the required attention, they perform all sorts of antics or stop in midstream like peeved and spoiled children and refuse to work at all. With all their arrogance the worst they can do is to let the boat drift. Out of this the passengers get a sort of unholy consolation as they watch these boisterous little slackers push their load back against the current just as far as they had allowed it to float out of its course. This according to the accepted laws of retribution is punishment enough for their willfulness.

But it is not so with those other ferries which are piloted across the river by strong cables stretched from one high tower to the other on opposite sides while the swiftly moving waters push the vessel across. The rigging by which this is done is not complicated but it has to be handled carefully if the navigator wants to avoid trouble. Fastened to a pulley which works on the master cable is a shorter one that is secured to the boat. This keeps it within the proper course. If the vessel is set at the proper angle with the current it floats steadily across to its destination. When the mechanism is properly handled it provides a very satisfactory means of navigation. But when in unskilled or careless hands it becomes a dangerous affair which may bring disaster to ship, crew, and cargo. Then the half mile or more between them and the shore and sixty or more feet between them and bottom becomes something to think about.

This latter situation is exactly what happened one Sunday during the spring roundup on the east side of the river. They were corralling at Muir's that week and the men, having come in early from their ride, decided to send several of the boys across to the store for some supplies. When they rode onto the boat they dropped their reins, found the most comfortable seats the rudely constructed craft could afford, and sat down to enjoy the trip.

The regular operator was an old-timer. He had spent all his life on the river. When he was a child the waters were his playmate. He played, also, in the hot sands and felt the stinging winds bite his cheeks when they blew cold from the mountains in wintertime and hot from the desert in summer. From the time Chief Joseph roamed over the plains with his tribe of Nez Perce Indians until the stockmen took possession he had crossed and recrossed this stream. Now he was old, his face was as brown and wrinkled as a baked potato, but his eye was keen, his body erect, and his hand steady. He loved his old, old friend, the Columbia! Passengers had no fear of that wild, turbulent monster when they were in the hands of the experienced old pilot.

But it so happened that his thirst sometimes overpowered him, at which times he would become completely incapacitated. For several days, they said, he had been gradually loading up and by now he was on the way under. By the time the boys wanted to return he was out. There was no one who would undertake to bring them back except a youngster who had often made the trip with the old captain but had never paid serious attention to the navigating equipment. He ventured to take the boat across, but he undertook more than he knew, and knew less than he pretended. The boys rode onto the deck, put up the bars, and turned their horses loose. They found good places to sit while the old ferry swung into the current. Set for sluggish waters, it slowly made its way out from the shore. The new pilot sat down to take his ease and gazed contentedly at the moving hills as the creaky thing put out toward midstream.

About forty rods from the shore the current became swift. This necessarily required a readjustment of the navigating apparatus, but the young navigator was sitting too comfortably to move. The rest of the men not knowing anything about the mechanism admired the swiftly moving stream, little thinking that it was planning to swallow them up. The first thing out of the ordinary that any of them noticed was an unusual creaking and straining at the cables, but they felt no alarm because they knew no better. They did not know that if the craft was set at a proper angle with a current the river would be their servant, and if not properly set it would draw them under.

They first became alarmed when they saw the water rising

up to the flat deck. They looked out over the river but there was no wind. Everything seemed to them as before only the boat was acting peculiarly. Now the water began to creep over the floor and the men sought refuge on the railing. The pilot was finally driven from his seat and sought to make adjustments of which he knew but little. But it was too late. The boat sank deeper and deeper. The men were now on the top railing where they sat astride an inch board with water all around them and the last part fast going down. The horses had been restless and were now becoming panicky and began to stampede until there was danger of crowding out the railing and all being swept away. Finally it began to tip and the last hope of the men was gone. Rough and untutored as most of them were, they now began to think about the things that usually come to people's minds when their last hope has disappeared. Then there was a snap and a whirring noise—the cable broke! The boat rose suddenly, and like a wild animal released from its confinement it frantically charted its own course downstream. The crew was without oar or rudder—nothing but a few poles which were used to pole the craft into position in the shallow waters at the landing places.

They were now careening wildly down the river like a tipsy sailor on shore leave and just released from jail. They glided on around the head of the butte, the village passed out of sight, and the island hid the corrals from view. As far as danger was concerned there was none unless their crazy craft should drift on a rock and rip a hole in its bottom as it accidentally might. There was no steering mechanism nor any landing equipment. "It's a long way to the Pacific," mused one of the buckaroos, "an' no one knows how to get this here critter corralled."

The next day when the Mountain Gem came steaming upstream it found an old man eagerly watching it from the time it first came into view far down the river. As it drew

114

nearer his dried and wrinkled face lit up with a smile. He saw his berserk runaway with all its cargo towed safely in the wake of this river steamer. Near Nagle's Landing miles away the current ran close to the shore. By tearing off boards from the ship's corral and using them for paddles they succeeded by hard work to bring the erstwhile truant to land. The next day when the Mountain Gem came along she picked them up and towed the whole outfit back to its owner.

The youthful navigator who was responsible for the trouble was no more trusted either by horsemen or by the old captain. His career as a river pilot had come to an untimely end. The cable was repaired and the ferry was again put into commission and made its way regularly across the stream.

The operator of the boat was old then. If he is still on duty he is older now—an old, old man. No doubt by this time he has made his last trip—not only over the Columbia, the river he loved from his childhood, but also over the stream from which no one ever returns. If so, let us hope that the cables held and that he made the harbor. There the Captain that piloted him across is safe and sure—He knows the way. When the vessel rocks, He holds it steady; when it sinks, He bids it rise. He has charted all the currents and fathomed the deep; He knows all the rocks and shoals. He controls every wind and rules every storm. When sunlight blackens into darkest night and the straining cables creak, above all the tumult there rises the comforting voice: "It is I; be not afraid."

"Here's where I love, the blue sky above
And the wide, open space,
The mounting plain, the guiding rein,
And the wind in my face.
To ride and rest, on the hill's high crest,
Under the open sky,
And to sleep without fear, when the stars are near,
And God close by."

Author Unknown

XII

A Fourth of July on the Plains

It was the third of July, just after we had become settled in our new home, when I rode over to the river headed for the horse corrals about ten or so miles from where the Columbia River cuts its way through the Saddle Mountains. I was looking for several work horses and had heard that the boys from the upper country had been corralling at Crab Creek and were delivering some stock at this place. Upon arrival I was informed that there were no horses available. So I turned homeward and rode until I found an empty cabin whose occupant had evidently left for the day— perhaps for several days. Being tired from the long ride, I picketed my saddle horse, prepared a supper of such things as I could find, and rolled in my blankets to sleep under the clear open sky. And such a sky! Who that has never seen it can comprehend the deep blue vault that stretches over the Great American Desert! A sky in which for days and weeks not a speck of cloud comes into view. During the heat of the day it appears an ashy gray, turning gradually into blue as the heat and light fade away. By eleven o'clock when darkness finally covers the land it is studded with millions of stars that seem to vie with each other in brilliancy. Compared with them those of the haze-filmed firmament of other lands look pale and almost lusterless. As I lay down in my blankets the last streaks of the fading light were reflected from the distant hills and fell on the earth like a benediction at the close of day. Such must have been the dry, cloudless vault into which the psalmist gazed from the hills of Palestine when he sang:

> The heavens declare the glory of God;
> And the firmament sheweth his handywork.

From the distance came the long, dreary howl of the coyote, the hoot of the desert owl, and the buzzing of the nighthawk's wings as he darted here and there after objects real or imaginary. Between these sounds pervaded the great stillness in which the Creator seems to hold communion with nature, the offspring of His hand. Amid such scenes and sounds and thoughts it was easy to fall asleep. As I gazed into the myriads of the shining host above I could well imagine why Jacob would dream of ladders that reached heavenward and of angels ascending and descending.

I was awake, however, to see the first streaks of dawn in the east—the dawn of the day that marked the anniversary of our nation's independence. Having exhausted the supply of water at the cabin the evening before I found it necessary to replenish my store in order to provide for the thirst of

118

the new day. I had learned by hard experience to take no risks when riding in the dust and heat for a stretch of ten hours or more. I saddled my horse and started for the river. After a ride of a quarter of a mile or so I reached the east bank which in those parts is almost perpendicular and in places more than four hundred feet high, and can be reached only by following stock trails to the water's edge.

Daylight was now sufficient to make things plainly visible. Before me and almost straight below me rolled the Oregon as Bryant called it, on its way to the sea. To the west rose the mountains, dark and blue. Still farther on and above all rose the snowy peaks of Adams and Ranier. Behind me lay the desert—covered with sagebrush, greasewood, and sunflowers—of which Kipling said, "Looks like a man long dead." It is true that the vegetation that lives here has little to commend itself to the admiration of passers-by, and yet one cannot but admire the brave and heroic struggle it puts forth to maintain its existence in such an unfriendly environment. When moisture is available it opens wide its arms to gather it in and make a quick new growth. Through the long hot days of summer when wind and sun vie with each other to bring about its destruction it closes up its pores securely and curls its little leaves tightly to conserve what moisture it has gathered during the snows and rains of winter.

Upon looking down to the water I spied an old bobcat lying on a projection of the rocks, unconscious that the eye of man, the disturber of nature, was on her. The last howl of the coyote as he was turning in for the day echoed and re-echoed from rock to rock and from hill to hill. A half mile or so up the river a band of wild horses that had evidently just come in from the range was leisurely taking a drink of the cooling water. Today they would lie in the shelter of the banks until the coolness of the night settled upon their world, then they would be off to the hills.

Such was the picture of nature unmarred by the hand of man. As I looked upon the scene and meditated my soul cried to the hills and mountains and the open sky, "Open your lips and tell me what has transpired here beneath your gaze in ages past. Where is the sea that once washed the shore high up on the mountainsides and lined it with shells and fossils and sand that were washed up from the deep? When did the earth open the doors to its interior and shoot forth its molten rock, red-hot, that flowed across these wide areas and left its craters deep in the bosom of the landscape?" Then from afar came the answer, "It is not for you to know the times or the seasons, but scenes such as you witness now are my masterpieces."

And from thee, old river, I have learned a lesson. After ages of beating and chopping thou hast cut thy way through yonder mountain and drained thy waters into the sea. But many, many times thy waves were broken upon the rocks before thy task was accomplished. And even now the waves which thou sendest out so bravely are often shattered and broken like the hopes of the soul. And yet over these same waves driftwood, and farther on large vessels carrying valuable cargoes, float into their desired haven.

So if after years of beating, which sometimes seem futile, I am able to remove the mountains that obstruct my way, I will be satisfied. But if I am not able to remove the barriers that confront me, and these shattered hopes of mine will provide the way over which others may be carried on to success, life will not have been lived in vain.

Then roll on Stream of Time to the sea of eternity, thy final resting place! What care I, after my course is run, whether I be carried swiftly away by the outgoing flood, or whether my spirit be buoyed for a season on the incoming tide, and I reach the sea, I know not how. Let this be my only care, that my soul may rise as the mist from the waters leaving sin and corruption and sorrow behind and ascend sanctified and pure into the presence of my Maker!

> And so beside the Silent Sea
>   I wait with muffled oar;
> No harm from him can come to me
>   On ocean or on shore.
>
> I know not where his islands lift
>   Their fronded palms in air;
> I only know I can not drift
>   Beyond his love and care.

> *Whittier*

Many foxes grow gray, but few grow good.

Benjamin Franklin

XIII

Outlaw Hogs

Some of the hay lands which the farmers and ranchers leased lay in the creek bottoms about twenty miles away from their home base. Each spring several men with teams were sent to clean out the ditches and get things in readiness for the summer irrigation. This meant weeks of disagreeable labor. Moving tons and tons of debris mixed with Russian thistles, broken boards and fence posts, tin cans and whatever else people dispose of by throwing it into the canals is not a pleasant task and no one was anxious for the job of cleaning up the mess. However, it had to be done; so a load of provisions was sent up to the place and several men were detailed to do the work.

They arrived at the sod shanty late one afternoon, and by the middle of the next day their house was set in order. It was cleaned after the fashion by which men clean house. The food was put on the shelves, beds were made up on the low bunks, and things were put in shape for cooking and sleeping. Scrapers were borrowed from a rancher up the creek and by the middle of the second day they were ready to begin moving dirt.

The old house in which they lived was a landmark in the community. It had survived, nobody knew how, many years of storm. The sod walls gave evidence of much wear and tear, and during times of wet weather the grass grew on the dirt roof as the psalmist says it did in Palestine or in other lands of similar climes. The windows were low and the broken panes were replaced with shingles and cardboard. As far back as settlers could remember this ancient soddy, it had looked very much the same.

During the greater part of the year it was unoccupied except by ground hogs and badgers that held forth under its creaky floor, and occasionally a skunk defied a would-be settler to dispossess her of her home. Sometimes travelers stopped for the night or to prepare meals en route through the country. At other times it was a lonely, decrepit little old place that was shown little respect or care. The wonder is that it survived so long, but like the rugged sons of the plain this humble remnant of someone's hope and ambition had a greater will to survive than did the one who dug up the sod for its walls and dirt-covered roof—he was gone to no one knew where.

Tradition connected this place with many episodes of doubtful veracity. Some people thought it was haunted. Those with active imagination spoke of mysterious lights moving around the building on dark and dismal nights at which times they said restless and uneasy spirits came forth out of their haunts. There were also stories of strange and uncanny sounds which made children hide under their covers when night came. Old-timers spoke of it having been a harbor or way station for cattle rustlers and outlaw gangs during the early days and of there having been some blood

124

spilled around the premises. But none of these reports could now be confirmed. In daytime it was just a simple, harmless cabin that had weathered the storms of the years, and all the imaginings of the fanciful died down when the prairie winds subsided and the sun shone again.

By now everybody looked upon it as a kind of roadside hostel to be occupied by anyone who cared to risk its crumbling walls that looked as though they were hardly able to carry the sod-covered roof. However, within a few days the men from the ranch had settled down to a routine that gave the place an air of occupancy. Early in the morning faint lights flickered like wandering ghosts between the shanty and the sheds. At noon the smoke curled skyward from the chimney and the smell of beans and soda biscuits and bacon brought home the hungry men without call from dinner horn or bell.

Among the inhabitants of that region was an old sow. No one seemed to know who owned her or where she came from. Her reputation was so notoriously bad that if anyone was responsible for her existence he would have hesitated to assert his claim in the presence of his much-outraged and greatly imposed upon and abused neighbors. The wonder is how she ever managed to survive. Her litter of pigs had grown almost as tall as she and what all of hoggish ingenuity and sagacity they had not inherited from their mother they had learned by experience. They were the dismay of the country around. Again and again the residents of the community declared that the spirit which possessed the herd of the Gergesenes by Galilee had taken up his abode in this one also.

The scattered settlers who lived within the range of her wanderings had suffered greatly from her depredations. Women saw their gardens uprooted and the fruits of their labor disappear. With many grunts of satisfaction long noses dug potatoes while settlers slept. Raiding chicken coops seemed to be their favorite pastime. The mother appeared to have had a kind of weird, mysterious way of knowing when people were gone from their homes. She took advantage of such situations and judging from her appearance and that of her family they were doing well. Men heaped upon them all the invectives of their language and sent loads of buckshot after the fleeing herd. Women set poison and dogs barked themselves hoarse, but their lives seemed charmed and they escaped every device designed for their destruction.

One day, however, they made a venture that almost resulted in their extermination. The men having finished their work had gone upcountry to return the scrapers they had borrowed. They planned to come back by noon, load their outfit, and start for home early next morning. It was during this absence that hunger or thirst or some more sinister motive prompted this farseeing mother with her brood to reconnoiter the vicinity of the sod shanty. Perhaps it was the smell of food that lured her on to make a thorough investigation of the place.

In some way, nobody knows how, she succeeded in getting the door open and gained admittance. Maybe it wasn't shut right—many people haven't learned the art of shutting doors. They leave all of them open as they pass through and then wonder why things happen. As a result of someone's carelessness or insecure locks and latches this source of community grief brought devastation to the larder of these hard-working, hungry men.

When this old mother and her family entered they no doubt saw at once that here was a feast all set and waiting for them. One movement of her overdeveloped snout sent the slop pail with its greasy contents rolling over the floor. Another haul landed the sack of flour in the midst of it, and still another sent all the contents of the shaky cupboard—lard and molasses, biscuits and bacon, beans and eggs and

126

whatever else there was—over the floor where it became accessible to her hilarious youngsters.

Then the whole family reveled in plenty. When they had taken their fill, true to their reputation, they wallowed in the residue. Judging from what one could see, they must have rubbed their sticky sides against the wall and bedposts and wiped their greasy snouts on blankets and bedding. Then they lay down to sleep off the effects of their carousal and festivity.

At this juncture the men returned, hungry and ready for their meal. They drove up to the sheds with sweet visions of pancakes and bacon and eggs. One of them hustled to the shanty to get dinner while the others unhitched and fed the team. On the way to the house the cook noticed that the door was open. As he drew closer he saw the old sow and her nefarious shoats around her, quietly settled and dozing away at the wall opposite the door. At once the prospect of a meal faded like a dream and the twenty miles between him and the home ranch loomed up like an endless road. He hastened back toward the sheds and shouted—in a subdued voice—"Say," he said, "the old sow is in the house and upset the cupboard."

"Shut the door and we'll butcher her!" came back the answer.

Here was his chance! At last this archenemy of the community was in his clutches and her dynasty was about to fall. In the next few minutes he gloated over the prospect of putting this neighborhood nuisance out of business by turning the whole herd into pork. This would not only yield them acceptable and much-desired provisions but would win him the approbation of the entire countryside. Already he was counting the hams, shoulders, and slabs of bacon and sausage and wondering how long this butchering job would delay their home-going. He sneaked up, seized the door, and slammed it shut. "How fortunate!" he thought.

The old desperado and her gang were finally trapped and headed for the meat block.

But the old brute was not so easily outdone. Her years had not been lived in vain and she was wise to all the ways of man—otherwise she could not have survived the murderous attempts upon her through all her days. She had evidently faced tight situations before and had learned what to do under such circumstances. The slamming of the door awakened her and the seriousness of the situation dawned upon her at once. A great "woof" brought every member of her family to its feet—wide awake! Then she made a swift lunge for the window which was much too small for her huge form; so she stuck. However, the impact of her weight carried her through and the end of the wall collapsed, while she galloped off across the prairie with her head in a frame, followed by her youngsters at a speed that vanquished every hope of fresh meat.

The old soddy which had harbored the community ghosts and furnished its imaginative residents with exciting topics of conversation was destined for the rubble heap. No more would it shelter fugitives or house wayfaring men or ranch hands who came to clean out irrigating ditches! Defeated and not a little chagrined, the men gathered up what was left of their outfit and drove twenty more miles to supper.

Where now these mingled ruins lie
    A shelter once to travelers rose,
Beneath whose roof with rafters high
    Full many a guest forgot his woes.

No more these walls by weather worn
    Afford the wanderer a safe retreat;
But night owls here, with eye forlorn,
    And slinking coyotes now will meet.

128

The friendly host whose kindly hand
  Greeted strangers at the door,
Hath left at last his wonted stand,
  And meets the coming guests no more.

Old creeping Time that brings decay
  Might well have spared these moldering walls,
Alike beneath whose potent sway
  A temple or a "soddy" falls.

Ye tyrant winds whose ruffian blasts
  Through doors and windows blows too strong,
And walls and roof to ruins casts
  The house that sheltered us so long.

Adapted from Philip Freneau's Stanzas Occasioned by the Ruins of a Country Inn.

Brave old Mackenzie long has laid him down,
To rest beside the trail that bears his name.
A granite makes his monument,
The Northers moaning o'er the low divide
Go gently by his long deserted camps.

Walt Whitman

XIV

The Cabin Beside the Trail

Crash! The glass struck the floor in front of the bar in the Bar-Two Saloon and burst into a thousand pieces. Johnnie Tincup, a half-breed Chickasaw, was in an ugly mood. The pug-nosed bartender had made several uncomplimentary remarks that involved the integrity of Johnnie's brother who was the proprietor of Jess's Place, a rival thirst-quenching emporium across the street. Then with his Chickasaw blood at boiling point, Johnnie stepped up to the bar, ordered drinks for the houseful of carousing buckaroos, emptied his glass, threw it on the floor with a crash, and openly championed his brother's cause.

There had been bad feeling between these two places for some time—in fact, for a long time. Each house had its loyal defenders. Now things looked bad! Johnnie's men were loyal to him. They had followed in the herd from the ranch some sixty miles beyond the blue hills that lay to the west. During the months of the roundup they had built up a sizable thirst of which they were now taking care. This, together with the feeling between the proprietors of the saloons and their loyal henchmen, made a bad combination and created a situation with forebodings of trouble.

After the episode in the Bar-Two, Johnnie walked out into the middle of the street, unholstered, threw his hat on the ground, and challenged the town to come and get him. He was raised on that sort of thing. When he was a mere lad he rode the range for cattle in Texas and followed the trail herds of some of the big cattle companies to the railroads in Oklahoma, New Mexico, and shipping points in other states. He had mixed with men of the Pecos Valley, the Panhandle, and other places during the roaring 80's and 90's of the last century. So this was nothing new as far as he was concerned. In later years he with his Indian bride made his way north and westward to their present home in the shadow of the Blue Hills in the state of Washington.

Now this Texan was in trouble. The people of the town all knew him. They knew too that he was ordinarily a peaceable citizen and that when he sobered up he would be very meek and apologetic about his conduct. So his challenge went unheeded. The officers of the town were satisfied to take the easy way out and let the affair run its course. Some of the more timid souls hid behind the buildings and occasionally a face peered around the corner to see what was going on.

With his challenge unheeded he picked up his hat, holstered his Colts, and crossed the street to Jess's Place where the smoke-filled air was thick with challenges, threats, and all kinds of portents of evil. All day he was the central figure in the trouble and carousal. He and his followers stormed drinking places, cleared the streets, and in general held possession of the town. No one cared to mix with the lot of half-drunken buckaroos who had turned themselves loose and became more hilarious as their thirst was in the process of being quenched. For the most part such conduct was what the town expected when men came in from the range where they had had no companionship for weeks, maybe months, except horses, coyotes, and jack rabbits.

Johnnie kept up with the boys until far into the night.

Then after shooting out the lights along the street, they made for the corrals where the chuck wagon with their bedding rolls was stationed and bedded down for what the peaceable citizens hoped would be a sobering sleep.

But Johnnie didn't sleep well. Other things were bothering him. All spring he was not his usual self. He complained of headaches. His face was often flushed as though he were feverish. He was irritable and sometimes moody. His wife's pleadings that he should take care of himself went unheeded. It was roundup time, he said, and things were not going right. Hy, who was boss of the outfit, did not work his men the way Johnnie thought he should. Then on top of it all they wasted a bunch of good ones when they brought the herd in from the big pasture the morning when they started across the miles to the railroad. He saw them break away and scatter wildly over the range to their old grazing grounds. When he rode away he spoke rudely to his wife who was standing in the doorway of the ranch house watching them go. Now this troubled him. While tossing in his fitful slumber beside the chuck wagon he saw her in his dreams, a lovely Chickasaw half-breed—perhaps less. He had found her on a large estancia in what was earlier known as the Staked Plains of Texas when he was a young cowboy riding herd for a cattle company. She had been educated in a girls' school and was cultured and well trained. She could paint, and write, and sing, they said. She could also play beautifully but there was no instrument in the Tincup home; hence this gift along with her other accomplishments languished, except that of reading. But she preferred the vocabulary of the plains with its double negatives and expletives rather than the refined and correct language of the schools. When Texas became fenced in, they followed the trail northward and settled in the desert where he located a claim, built up a sizable herd of horses, and did some dry farming beneath the shelter of an overhanging coulee wall, where he built his house and stables and corrals.

The morning following his wild carousal he rose with a headache. He had no desire to join in further rivalry. He was humiliated and remorseful and wanted only to get back to his home. He filled his saddlebags with sardines, canned goods, and crackers—the staple rations of the plainsmen who have to travel light. Then he filled his water bag with water, turned the chuck wagon over to the trail boss, and started home alone.

As he rode along his headache increased and he felt sick all over. With the hot sun beating upon him and the glaring sandy plains before him, his head throbbed and at times his vision was so blurred that he could hardly see. He really had no more than started the long ride and he was already too ill to stay in the saddle. He realized that it was useless to try to make even a part of the trip.

But in all those miles there were not many places to stay. Ordinarily he would have stopped in the shadow of a coulee wall or even beside a sagebrush but now, with his mind reeling and his senses sometimes almost blotted out, he did not want to take chances by getting off the trail. He realized that he could not go on. Nor did he know how soon some of his men would be along and perhaps when they did come, they would not find him.

After a carousal such as he had the day before he always felt a letdown and now it didn't make much difference, he thought, what would happen. Life had been hard. He had had a struggle since boyhood to secure what he now owned. Others could round up those cayuses as well as he. But that wasn't what he was most concerned for—he wanted to see his wife—her saddened face haunted him.

As he rode along he recalled that there was a deserted cabin to the left of the trail. Some years earlier it had been occupied by a nester who no doubt hoped to make a farm out of this patch of sun-parched, wind-blown desert land and had failed. After a hard ride, during part of which he hardly knew where he was going, he drew up beside the shack, dismounted, tied his horse to a sagebrush, staggered to the door, and looked in. The place was empty except for the rudely constructed bunk in the far corner. At the other end there was a little stove, and several boxes lay scattered over the floor. He cared for nothing except for a place to lie down. He spread his bed roll on the bunk, hung his water bag where he could reach it, lay down, and fell asleep.

Once during the night he was awake. The big round moon was shining through the window. He was so sick he could hardly move. He sipped some water from his waterbag to cool his fevered body and fell asleep. When he woke up the sun was shining on the floor of the shanty. He was hot and his head throbbed as though it would burst. He staggered to the door thinking to mount his horse and resume his long ride home, but he failed. He made his way back to his bunk and when occasionally his mind cleared, he was worried about himself. People seldom passed along this trail and if they did, it was not probable that any of them would go out of their way to stop at this deserted place.

He was too sick now to care much whether he lived or died. He wondered what was wrong with him. Perhaps, he thought, his fever was caused by the water he drank from a ditch during the roundup weeks earlier. He tried to rise to his feet but this time his limbs refused to carry him. He sank back into his bunk and lay there the rest of the day. Sometimes he slept. When he was awake his mind cleared occasionally, then the cloud overshadowed him and he was in dreamland where he saw his wife standing in the doorway, her eyes shielded with her hand against the sun, looking across the wide spaces from which she knew he would return.

Once when he was awake and conscious he noticed that

135

he had left the door open. What if wild beasts should come in! There were bobcats and rattlesnakes and other varmints on these plains and he was not in condition to defend himself against any of them now. He tried again to get to his feet and close the door but could not. His last recollection of the day was that it was beginning to get dark, then memory fell away and he was asleep. When he awoke the sun was again shining on the floor. Was this the same day, he wondered, or was it the next day or how many days had passed since he came here? He managed to get his water bag and drink. Again he fell asleep. In his dreams he saw animals around him. Beasts came in the open door and snakes—rattlesnakes. He fought them all!

When he woke up the sun was once more shining in the window. On the other side of the room against the wall lay a huge rattler that had crawled in out of the sun and was staring at him with its beady eyes. He tried to get his water bag but his hands fell limp to his side. Sometimes he fancied he saw his wife but when he reached for her, she was gone. Then again his disordered thoughts wandered to the range where he was a king among the horsemen.

Several days after the carousal the trail boss gathered up the outfit and started for the Running W. The boys drifted out of town in small groups of twos or threes on their way back to the ranch. The sun beat upon them; the dust rose out of their tracks and hung lazily upon their trail. They noticed a lone horse standing outside the cabin to their left. Their knowledge of desert life told them that it was not a range horse. He would not stand for any length of time on the sunny side of the house. Then, too, it looked as though he were saddled; so they decided to ride over and see who was holding forth at this deserted place.

As they approached they recognized the horse as belonging to their boss. He was gaunt and looked as though he was hardly able to stand. He had had no water since he was tied here and no feed except what he could reach from the end of the rope. The saddlebags and lariat were still in their places on the saddle. Marks on the ground indicated that he had been standing there for several days. Then they looked inside the cabin. In the corner lay Johnnie, his eyes and his cheeks sunken and his hair matted.

"Looks like the boss is 'bout ready for kingdom come," said one. "Shure does," commented the other. Usually these buckaroos got their theological terminology badly garbled but this time they were not far off.

His breathing was easy now. Large drops of sweat stood on his face and his body felt cool and clammy. Here was their old friend, one of the strong men of the range! He was rough on the outside and sometimes stern when he was boss of the roundup. They couldn't let him die, they said, without an effort to help him. These crude sons of the wild would do that for their worst enemy. Bill rode back to the railroad for a doctor. Shorty went to the ranch to get his wife.

Once more Johnnie opened his eyes. He was still alone. The sun still shone on the floor. He looked at his water bag but cared no more for it. His body seemed cool now. He fell asleep again. In his dreams he walked through beautiful fields, by cooling waters, among shady trees. His wife was with him. The saddened look on her face was gone.

When the doctor came he stepped inside and made an examination of his patient who was still in dreamland. One thing he knew. The man had had a violent fever, but now he was exhausted and weak and it appeared as though his life was about burned out. One of the men said soberly in the language of the plains that "Johnnie is 'bout to turn his toes to the daisies." The wild carousal and the ride through the hot sun had done him no good. But the fever was gone and Johnnie was about gone too. No, he could not be moved, the doctor said, and there was hardly a chance that he would recover. He left some medicine, gave directions for his care, and left the patient in the hands of Bill.

In the door of the ranch house at the Running W stood a trim, slender woman looking across the plains to the northeast. She had been watching in that direction for days. Now that a streak of dust was rising along the trail she was sure that Johnnie was coming home. This had been a long, hard wait. He had often been out of patience with his men, but he had never spoken to her as he did the morning when he and his men started for the railroad with the horses. She knew this had been a hard season for him. He had not been well and many things had gone wrong. She felt sure that he would soon be at home. She prepared his meal and got herself ready to go to the corral to meet him.

As the horseman rounded the hill at the mouth of the coulee she saw that it was not Johnnie, but Shorty from the ranch over at the river. She knew him well. He rode for them the past several years during the roundup. As he dismounted at the corral gate she saw that there was something wrong. When she met him he told her the story of the condition in which they had found her husband. He was "he'pless and he was breathin'," Shorty said, "but he didn't talk none." He said his body was cool and clammy but he was still alive. Bill had gone for the doctor, he told her, and he had come to get her.

The dusk of the evening was already gathering when the buckboard with Johnnie's wife sitting beside the driver left the ranch house and drove past the corral into the gathering dusk, headed for the cabin beside the trail where her husband lay. It was a long drive. Once during the night they stopped at a spring to feed the team and prepare a pot of coffee. Then they were off again. Would he be alive when she got there? she wondered. Could he speak to her or could she speak to him? She saw him again, his lithe form, his browned face with a sprinkling of gray in his hair. He was

138

rough and ready and had always been able to take care of himself and make his way. Almost from childhood he had battled against circumstances and won. But now he was helpless and perhaps would be beyond any aid she could give.

In midforenoon the next day the buckboard drew up at the little shanty. The woman dismounted. Bill sat on a box outside the door and nodded to her inquiry as to whether her husband was still living. She stepped inside—there in the corner he lay. She went up to the bed and laid her hand on his clammy forehead, but there was no response. She stood beside him as one in a trance, looking at the wasted form before her. She did not move until Shorty came to the door and inquired whether there was anything he could do. Then she got water, washed his hands and face, and sponged his body as best she could. She combed his matted hair and did what she thought would make him comfortable.

Then followed lonely days of waiting. The nights were cool as desert nights are, but in the daytime the sun beat unmercifully upon the roof of the cabin. Sometimes she was hopeful and again she despaired. When she spoke there was no answer. Yet he lived on and somehow she felt he would get well. One morning he opened his eyes and looked around. The sun was shining on the floor and his wife was standing beside the bunk. Gradually his strength came back. One day they carried him to the buckboard and took him home. After several months he was "hisse'f" again and loitered around the ranch until the fall roundup, then he was in the saddle as of yore.

It was some time before Johnnie Tincup went to town again. But gradually he made it. That fall when school opened he moved to his small ranch close to town. It was during this time that I went to the Running W to help with the stock. They were doing some light riding among the buttes and coulees and scab rock—lava lands—for some of his horses. This was a wonderful experience for me. To ride to the top of one of these great bluffs and look for miles in every direction was a real inspiration. Horses grazing in the valley looked like pygmies from where I sat in the saddle and beheld the glory of my surroundings.

Meanwhile changes had taken place in the little frontier town. Gamblers, bunko men, loose women, and the riffraff from here and there had drifted in. The cabins that lined the high enclosures behind the drinking emporiums were all occupied by shady females who hung over the bar and preyed upon the men that sat at the faro or card tables with the chips stacked high.

One day Johnnie and I rode to town. He wanted to get someone to mow weeds which had grown up during the summer and were threatening to smother the place. I wanted to get the mail. After loafing a while he crossed over to the Bar-Two where Dutch Charley was sitting on the steps, bleary-eyed, with all inhibition gone. He sat down beside him and tried to persuade him to come out to the ranch and clean up the weeds. Dutch Charley was very frank and informed his would-be employer that "he wouldn't work for him at no price." He didn't "trust no Tincup none." Jess, Johnnie's brother, so Charley said, had robbed him and that was to be the end of his dealing with those varmints. That was more than Johnnie could take.

When I returned from the post office my eyes followed along the opposite side of the street to locate the pair that had seemed to get along so well a few minutes earlier. I found them in the middle of the street with the Dutchman on his hands and knees trying to get up while Johnnie rained blows upon his head to prevent it. Charley's face was bloody and Johnnie was mad. He went in to Jess's Place and began to "liker-up." Then everybody got ready for a street clearing and other incidentals, the consequences of which no one would venture to predict.

But other things had happened also. The influx of the bad element had led the city fathers to hire a new town marshal. He was a tall, lanky, slope-shouldered, bow-legged fellow that was anything but an imposing figure in the law enforcement department. When he found that the town had no jail, he declined the offer of the position. "No one can't keep no order," he said, "without a calaboose." To construct a jail that would hold the type of occupants that would likely inhabit the place required more money than the town had to spend. So they located a cook shack which was built on the running gears of a wagon and decided that it could be reinforced to hold what it was expected to hold. Besides, it had the advantage of being on wheels and if the candidates for admission to its quarters were difficult to move, the jail could be taken to the place where they were and they could be loaded up with a minimum of trouble.

After the appropriate amount of glassware had been smashed and much talk had been made, Johnnie went out on the street as his custom was. In the meantime word was passed around that he was "likering-up" at Jess's Place and was "making gun talk" agin the proprietor of the Two-Bar and its friends. This rival of his brother's place always was an annoyance to him and affected him like barbwire in a turkey's gizzard, as the saying was among the buckaroos.

This time, however, he went without hardware. He had left his own at home and the boys would loan him none. That aggravated him all the more. His own men were not with him. With his sombrero on the ground beside him he stood in the street heaping vengeance upon the Two-Bar, embellished with all the invectives of his ample vocabulary. His arm was raised to an angle of about forty-five degrees with his trigger finger pointing skyward. In his speech he included all the people in the house except the ladies. To talk disparagingly of a woman was not good Chickasaw ethics, in which Johnnie was deeply versed.

The new marshal stood a few doors down the street and took in the proceedings. People had much to say about the amount of daylight that went between his spindly bowlegs and they were not sure that he was equal to situations such as he was now facing. He moved leisurely up to Jess's Place, went in, and disarmed himself. He unbuckled his holster, and hung it up behind the bar. Then he went out to get his man. As he approached him, his eyes narrowed until they were mere slits. Johnnie warned, "Don't you tech me. Don't you lay no hand on me." But the marshal went on, took him by the arm, led him to the portable calaboose, and locked him up. The next morning he was brought before the court, fined, and released.

That was Johnnie's Waterloo! He went home a humbled and defeated man. Not only was he cowed and humiliated but the array of gamblers, sports, bad men and women also took the cue and moved on. The new marshal had made his record and was in control of the situation. How all this happened is still a mystery. I presume the spirit of the old west had petered out.

After we left the country I heard nothing of Johnnie Tincup until only a few years ago. I was then informed that in his latter years he moved to the Yakima country and settled down to a quieter life. I have a faint recollection—so faint that I do not entirely trust it—that he reformed, "joined up" with a church, and became a peaceable and God-fearing citizen. If so, then I hope to meet him again at the end of the trail after it crosses the Great Divide—this greathearted child of the horse country who was always so kind to me!

Perhaps during his last years Johnnie lived in the spirit of the song of the plainsman who had found the **Way**:

> Last night as I lay on the prairie
> Looking up at the stars in the sky,
> I wondered if ever a cowboy
> Could go to that sweet bye and bye.

Someday there will be a grand roundup,
Where cowboys like cattle will stand
To be cut out by the Riders of Judgment
Who are posted and know every brand.

The road that leads down to perdition
Is posted and blazed all the way,
But the pathway that leads up to heaven
Is narrow and dim, so they say.

Whose fault is it then that so many
Go out on that wide range and fail,
Who might have honor and plenty,
Had they known of that dim, narrow trail.

Author Unknown

. . . and after the fire
a still small voice.

I Kings 19:12

XV

Breaking Camp

We liked the sagebrush country, the land to which we came to find a home. When we left Iowa we little dreamed what all was involved in making the change from a socially and religiously stable community to settling down in a place where everything is more or less in a flux. With the exception of the old-timers the country was occupied by people who had broken with the old and had not permanently found themselves in the new situation. There was much shifting of the population. People moved hither and yon looking for something better than they had thus far found. After a brief stay some of the immigrants that had come to the new country so enthusiastically and full of hope returned to their former homes in the east because life in these undeveloped sections was too hard. Others were disappointed with the dust and the dry rainless months, and the wind and heat. Some discovered that they had been caught by the real-estate sharks and had paid their money for something that was almost worthless. Then they went back east with a bad opinion of all thy had seen or heard.

But we liked the country. Its climate was for the most part delightful, except during the months of July and August when the heat was at its worst, and even then the nights were cool. We enjoyed the vast open spaces, the wild unsubdued environment, much of which had not been marred or tampered with by the hand of man. The ever-changing mountain scenery kept us enthralled all the time. When the atmosphere was clear the snowy line along the horizon marked the boundary between earth and sky. During the hot summer they were smoke-dimmed and hazy much of the time and furnished the eyes, desert bruised and weary, with a resting place from the glare of the sandy plain.

In its natural state the country is more or less barren and unproductive. Its scanty grasses furnish feed for roving stock and in the higher altitudes vast wheat fields stretch for miles on every side. In other places irrigation systems have carried water to the land and as if by magic orchards and groves, fruits and flowers have leaped from the soil and made the barrens blossom and bloom in the richness of their fruit-age. In the hot summers the shimmering heat waves played tricks with a person's vision. One sometimes saw cities in the clouds, or beautiful lakes in the distance where there was nothing but sagebrush and sand. Whatever there was in the way of life or vegetation often assumed weird and at times frightening forms as the heat waves frolicked with the desert atmosphere.

In the spring when the earth reflected the rays of the oncoming summer sun air columns were set in motion that swept the land and sent up clouds of dust that virtually turned the daylight hours into twilight. Then when the rain came, as it sometimes did, the aroma of the toasted earth ascended skyward as a pleasing odor of adoration to its Maker.

But there were some things that we missed. Of these, church privileges and the possibility of church attendance were the most important. During our year's residence in Prosser we attended public worship at such places as were available. With many of these frontier folks, religious life was a halfhearted affair, lacking greatly in enthusiasm and sincere devotion. This was not the fault of the churches but rather the result of the indifference of the community that was much older than its religious interests and activities.

After moving to the ranch the closest places of worship were twenty miles away. Attendance was clearly out of the question. A few times a convalescing missionary from India who had come to this region hoping to regain his health conducted services in our home. Only once during our residence in this section did I have the opportunity of attending an evening service at one of the churches while I was detained in town during a freighting trip. As I think of it now as the pastor of that indifferent flock surely deserved the commendation of his associates and superiors for his forbearance, patience, and fortitude in staying with what was then a most unpromising and uninspiring situation.

Educational advantages were far removed. There were no children in our section of the country. In other places where there were, the parents moved to the towns or villages where school privileges were available. This accounted for housing developments of the most primitive order, such as Chickasaw Flat in the town where we did our trading. Many of the occupants were more or less temporary. The population usually was a mixture of all the country had and included well-to-do and poor, the well-kept together with the unwashed and uncombed, and the old and young. Each family had its collection of hound-dogs, cats, and sundry other animals with which they shared their food and housing. When spring came and school closed many of them returned to their holdings. Some stayed on throughout the year. During the harvest the men followed the wheat and grain fields and threshing outfits until the season was over, then they returned as regularly as the birds go to their winter homes.

The social life of the country was meager. It consisted mostly of calls and visits of settlers who, en route to some engagement, stopped for a meal or the exchange of such news as filtered in across the sandy plains. Occasionally the people would get together along the bluffs of the Columbia for an outing where meat, sometimes jack rabbit or sage hens, would be roasted, and the coffee was boiled on a sagebrush fire. More rarely yet some socially minded family would invite the surrounding people to their home for an evening of such entertainment as they were able to provide in their meager dwellings.

In spite of the lack of opportunity along social and religious lines, those were happy days. People lived far enough apart and saw so little of each other that they were always glad for meetings along the way. Many of the homesteaders had the merest kind of shacks to live in and had no way of getting from place to place except by walking. A few had saddle horses and fewer yet had other transportation facilities. The miles which lay between the occupants of the range naturally limited the social activities of the community.

One time one of the enterprising homesteaders conceived the idea of converting a small cabin into a grocery store and post office, and after much negotiating with the Federal authorities at Washington, D.C., Wheatly became established with the wife of one of the settlers as postmistress. Their remuneration for carrying the mail over the sixteen miles to and from the railroad was to be derived from the sale of postage stamps. But the letter writers were few; hence the income of the postmistress was pitifully meager. The grocery and notion sales were certainly not burdensome and the profits were small. After a year, perhaps less, Wheatly was discontinued when the proprietor of the little store relinquished his connection with the ranch and moved to his claim which lay along the top of White Bluff overlooking the Columbia River.

The residence on a large ranch was really the only structure on Sunflower or Columbia Flat that deserved the dignity of being considered a house. A son of the owner was to be the proprietor. He had been educated at one of the large colleges of the East and came to this section of the country to become a wheat farmer. When their buildings were completed, the well dug, and the pumping equipment installed, the occasion was celebrated with the most elaborate social affair in the history of that part of the country. All the schoolteachers who had left their posts of duty in the various cities and towns of the state, the buckaroos and homesteaders, wheat ranchers and some of the society folks from a distance were present to participate in the frolic. It was a gala affair. Lithe girls and obese matrons bespangled and bedangled with jewels and pearls, lassies from the Purple Sage and country women glided across the floor on the arms of the "knights of the saddle" with spurs ajingling, or with whosoever was available as an escort. This was the grandest, the only, and the final function of its kind during our residence in those parts. It was both the opening and closing event of the social season and of all seasons as far as we know.

Later the manager brought his bride, a lovely girl, from an eastern town to the ranch to become the mistress of their domain. No doubt she had looked forward with much anti-

cipation to the many thrills of western life and it may easily
have been that she was considered the heroine of the gay
social set in which she moved, many of whom may have
envied her this experience.

But after she had covered by buckboard the dusty miles
from the railroad to her new home, endured the burning
summer heat for the few short weeks of her stay, smelled
the sagebrush, and scanned the ocean of desert and the
limitless, barren sky her short-lived enthusiasm disappeared.
A person could hardly have expected anything else and
certainly no one blamed her. Then she returned to her
eastern home and her spouse retired from his venture in
wheat growing and took up the work of the profession for
which he had been trained. He was a good friend of ours
and we hated to see him leave. The social life of the desert
which had such an auspicious beginning suffered a severe
setback and had a very drab and uninteresting demise without even the proper obsequies. Adios! social life on
Columbia Flat.

But in spite of the disadvantages and hardships, the place
to which we had come was so intriguing that we might still
be there had not a Guiding Hand which shapes one's destiny
reached into our affairs and directed our paths. One fall my
wife's brother went back to the old home in Iowa for a
visit. While there he became ill and died. The message came
to us on Christmas when we had invited some of the men to
our cabin for dinner. How well we remember the day! A
quiet rain was softly falling when a messenger from the
telegraph office twenty miles away rode up to our door with
a telegram announcing the death, the first one in the family.
The next day we drove across the long miles to the railroad,
where my wife and our little boy took the train for home.

That visit stirred something within her that had laid
dormant for some years. After she came back from her trip
we both felt that perhaps for our own good and for that of

150

our child we should return to a more settled community. We realized that this country, though interesting and inspiring, was no place for youngsters to grow up. As mature people we thought we could survive, spiritually and physically, but not so with children. The manner of our life had its roots deep in the teachings of the Gospel and even in my association with all kinds of men with whom I worked these convictions held and carried me through. We decided to find some place to live where we could enjoy the good things we lacked here in the desert and at the same time live in an environment where the spirit of the westland remained.

During the following summer we began to dispose of our stock and other chattels and got ourselves ready to leave. In July my family left. I stayed until sometime in the month of October in order to finally prove up on the land we had homesteaded and settle up such other business as there was. In addition to our own affairs there was my deceased brother-in-law's estate to be probated and cleared up before I could get away. All of this required time and kept me in the country longer than I had anticipated.

But it proved to be a pleasant time. All of our stock had been disposed of except Babe, our favorite saddle horse. There were no longer contracts to fulfill, no responsibility to carry, and no work to do except to prepare my meals and keep the cabin clean. I was merely biding time and doing the things that had to be done which were few.

It was then that I became aware of how deeply we had become attached to our home on the range. What few settlers there were who braved the summer's heat to stay on their claims called at our cabin for a last word. Stockmen who straggled across the country on various errands stopped as they went by and ate with me my soda biscuits, johnnycakes, bacon and beans and drank a brew that passed for coffee. It was election year and my good friends offered me the nomination for treasurership of the county which

151

was then about as large as the state of Rhode Island. Other tempting offers were made which would surely have been difficult to turn down if my family had still been with me.

All these manifestations of good will, together with the quiet restfulness of my surroundings, seemed to hold me closely to the place. Memories rose out of the past on every side and I found myself bound by ties which I had not known to exist. But the die was cast! The Hand that unfailingly leads one on to the divinely appointed plan for his life, if one is willing to follow His leading, had taken over and was directing my course.

But we had become so enamored with the spirit of the thinly occupied spaces that neither of us—my wife or I— wanted to settle down in the thickly populated, convention-laden, and tradition-bound communities we had known before. We then compromised and decided to locate on the western end of the Great Plains in the panhandle of Nebraska, where we felt that the spirit of the west remained and where there was a little congregation of the faith which was deeply implanted into our lives from our early childhood.

Here in this little church I heard the Master's call to the ministry and took charge as its pastor. After several years of service in this community the bishop of the home church in southeastern Iowa, where we were married and where both of us had become Christians and were baptized, invited us to return and assist in the pastoral work of that congregation. From there the same Hand led into other and larger fields of service that since then have occupied my time and blessed my years with the assurance that "all things," even life along the horse trails, "work together for good to them that love God, to them who are the called according to his purpose." I see now the wisdom of God in permitting His chosen and called ones to walk the paths on the back side of the desert in order to prepare them for His service. Those

152

years were hard but they were rich in providing materials for use in my ministry. They were also a potent force in mellowing my character, and maturing my life for the duties that later were to be mine.

Since then the way has not been easy but it was always sure. Nor has the yoke always been light. But through the years we found that we do not need to bear our burdens alone. We also learned in a small measure to possess our souls in patience and have found that "the Lord's mercies ... are new every morning."

We discovered that the desert is not only a vast sweep of land and sagebrush but also a place of rest for jaded bodies and minds. How often the spirit of the primitive wild, where quietness and restfulness brooded over tired souls, opened wide its arms and invited me into its embrace! Here I could disentangle myself from the problems that threatened to drag me down, and, after days of refreshment and reflection within the soothing peacefulness of these surroundings, I again saw clearly the way that the Master chose for me. Then I returned to my duties in the busy world and resolved anew to abide in His will and do His bidding until the sun sets on the trail and the morning breaks over the "land that is fairer than day."

As one who walking in the twilight gloom,
Hears 'round him voices as it darkens,
  And seeing not the forms from which they come,
Pauses from time to time and hearkens.

Henry Wadsworth Longfellow

XVI

People of the Desert

Oftentimes when "the hours of the day are numbered" I see again in the gathering twilight the shadowy forms of the people we knew and lived with during our residence in Sagebrush Land. In the quiet hours when the cares of the day drop away they—our friends and neighbors—come to visit us once more. I see them now as they were when I saw them last, almost a lifetime ago.

They were children of the Old West, the fading remnant of a group drawn from a rugged but famed period of America's history. They constituted a heterogeneous group which the winds had blown together from the four corners. Among them were the young and strong who were ready to face any task. There were also those whom the years had matured and seasoned, who faced life with mellowed judgment and discretion. And there were the aged and weatherworn who lingered in the shadows of the past, many of them uncertain of where the trail leads to from here. There were also the untutored and unlearned, the well-trained and highly educated, some of whom had been successful in their professions, business, and other occupations in which they had served. They were religious in their own way. Their thinking had been touched only remotely by the churches to which many of them were strangers. They were helpful, kind, and considerate. Many of them were old-timers who had reached the country before the advent of the law and had followed their own moral and legal code. On the whole they were law-abiding citizens and good neighbors.

Today they are still my friends though they are by this time widely scattered and no doubt many of them have come to the end of the road and have "turned in" their saddles and spurs. But tonight in my reverie it seems that I hear the well-known sounds of long ago coming out of the past. There is the clatter of hoofs on the scab rock, the creaking of the wheels of the trail wagon, and the chatter of familiar voices. It must be that they are on the move again—here they come!

Henry Gable, the Horseman

He was perhaps the most interesting of all these men. I never could find out where he came from. There were stories that he came from the East. One of the most appealing of these traditions was that he was one of the two who years earlier emerged one evening from one of the mountain passes on the east side of the Great American Desert that stretched away before them to the west until it passed beyond the range of human vision. There he and his companion halted their pack train and shielding their eyes against the sun, looked out over that vast expanse into the shadows of the afternoon. They had come westward seeking an unoccupied range for stock.

One of them looking over that dry, sandy waste dotted with sagebrush, greasewood, and dried-up sunflowers that covered the miles as far as the eye could see, shook his head and said, "What a desolate and barren waste!" No doubt he was disappointed and wondered, like other newcomers, how a person could survive in a place like this. The other one looked over the same vast expanse and said, "No! This is a horse country." Acting upon that faith he pushed inland and pitched his tent on the rim of an ancient volcano which long ago spent its force. Nature had by this time sealed up its mouth, leaving only an ugly hole on the face of the landscape. Here he erected his cabin and set up his business. A corral was built on the floor of the crater. Stock trails zigzagged back and forth in a shuttlelike fashion from top to bottom on the north slope to a pool of water, deep in the hollow, fed by perennial springs that finally drained into a subterranean stream through a cleft in the steep, rocky wall on the south side.

The small herd which he brought with him did not consist of the cayuse or ordinary range type of horses. His stock was headed by a good sire that was to perpetuate the quality that marked and distinguished the holdings of the Bracket H outfit throughout its history. They grazed on the large open range which then extended from the Snake River on the south to the Okanogan country on the north. Over the years that followed wheat ranchers and irrigation projects cut across the grazing land and broke it into isolated parts. During our day his horses roamed from the Columbia eastward and north beyond the Saddle Mountains into and beyond the Moses Lake country. Scattered bands were reported to have been found far beyond these bounds.

So true had been the vision of this young adventurer that he prospered. His herds increased until the Bracket H horses were known far and wide and Gable was known not only for his stock but also for his honesty and integrity.

A few days before I left the country for good I rode over to Scootney Springs, his headquarters, to make arrangements about a few head of cayuses I was leaving on the range. He and one of his men were sitting outside their cabin mending lariats and riding gear. The shadows of evening were gathering when I left. This was the last time I visited his place. As I write I see him again astride his horse, leaning on the horn of his saddle and looking into the fading day. He was an old weather-beaten man, a symbol of the Old West that was then on the way out.

When after a few years following my departure from this part of the country this Prince of Horsemen "turned in his spurs," no doubt many of the stockmen and ranchers whom he had befriended came to his last "roundup." During my visit to the old range this past summer (1954) after an absence of forty-six years, I learned that no one seems to know where he lies buried. Some of the old-timers think that he was taken to the town by the railroad and laid to rest in the cemetery. One of them said, "No one knows where he came from and no one seems to know where he went!" I like to think that perhaps his friends and associates of the range wrapped him in his blankets, pillowed his head on his saddle from which he surveyed his domain for years, and laid him away by the fountain to which the vision of his youth had led him.

Today Henry Gable's range is gone. The "Bracket H" horses that once roamed far and wide over the desert are gone too—no one seems to know where they went! Wide canals now carry water to the thirsty land which is criss-crossed with miles and miles of paved roads and covered with fields of grain, budding orchards, and thousands of homes where in his time there were only horse trails, sagebrush, and greasewood and cabins around which the wind swept in daytime and at eventide coyotes put the world to sleep with their doleful howls.

Men of the River

The earliest settlers in this area were the rivermen among whom were traders that established posts along the watercourses and traded with the Indians and others who went up and down the stream. Some of them were adventurers who loved the solitude, the great desert, and the blue mountains. Others followed the stock business and still others took up plots of land where water for irrigation was available and built up simple homes surrounded by trees and vines and little fields of alfalfa for their few cayuses or a few head of cattle. Their needs were not many. Their lives were free from the complexities that one finds in the more densely settled communities.

Among these old-timers was a man named Muir. If he had a given name it has completely eluded my memory by now. He was one of those who took up land along the river. He had a few cattle, some horses, and freighting equipment, and cultivated a little ground. He was a trader and bought and sold whatever was to be had and was needed by the settlers, ranchers, travellers, and Indians.

He was an adventurous soul and enjoyed the water. In the spring he gathered up his logging equipment and drove overland to the mountains which lay northward along the Columbia where the timber grew. There he established camp and with his crew felled the trees, cut them into suitable lengths, floated or hauled them to the banks of the river, and built them into a mammoth raft. This then became a large float upon which he loaded his outfit—horses, wagons, and all—set up his tent, and sailed down the stream to his holdings miles below Priest Rapids. There in his primitive sawmill logs were turned into lumber, the poles into fence posts, railing for corrals, or whatever else was needed by the sparse population that occupied the country.

The trip down the river was the dream of his existence. For days the raft glided through gorgeous mountain passes, or past the orchards in the irrigated sections, or along the wheat fields where isolated ranchers braved the vicissitudes that befell the farmer and husbandman in that section.

But there were also rapids, steep and swift, that had to be run. By far the most dangerous were the Priest Rapids at the point where the river cut its way through the Saddle Mountains. Here the waters boiled and roared over the miles that led to the more tranquil flows below.

To maneuver his raft through the maze of rock over which the wild waters raced was a task that challenged all the skill, judgment, ingenuity, and wisdom that he had. Once his raft went to pieces when it hit one of the ledges and the logs went careening madly through the watery waste. His team, outfit, and equipment were lost, but he being a child of the river made his way through the raging torrent to safety. His men sometimes spoke of the tenseness that overtook him as they approached the rapids but once they entered them a coolness that is born of emergency overtook him as he guided his cargo through to safety. Then he virtually collapsed from exhaustion after they had floated into the placid waters and slept for hours on end for the rest of the way.

An Engineer Who Dreamed

Late in the first decade of the present century I sat on my horse on the White Bluffs high above the Columbia and saw from my saddle the Mountain Gem plowing its way upstream on its maiden voyage. Its decks were crowded with passengers who lined the railing to enjoy the majesty of the stream and the varied scenery along the way. Here and there bands of wild, free horses were lounging along the river's edge for a last quaff of water before starting on their long trek across the plateau in quest of food. The scattered little patches of irrigated lands with vine-embowered huts and houses surrounded with trees and

160

shrubs and flowers brought to them a breath of freshness to break the monotony of the desert along the way. Added to the color of the purple sage (to some of us it looked gray) was the blue haze that bedecked the mountains in the distance and above it the ashen sky that looked hot during the day but which became cool and refreshing as the stars twinkled into view with the fall of the night when the breezes blew cool fron the snow peaks.

It is said that when the Mountain Gem stopped at the foot of the roaring Priest Rapids the captain swore and said that if it were not for that barrier which blocked his way he could take his craft far upstream through the deep gorges where the river cut its channel through the mountains, whose steep slopes were covered with the growth of the massive pines and cedars and firs. There rhododendrons and other flowers bloomed in glorious array when the snows retreated before the onslaught of the summer sun.

But one day a young engineer passed that way. When he beheld that same wild, roaring mass of water tumbling down over the steep incline of the rapids he became enthralled with its possibilities and cried, "Here lies the strength of a million horses! Someday I'll harness this energy and hitch it to the wheels of commerce. I'll make it turn the machinery of the mills and mines, light the streets of the city, the homes of the villages and the countryside, and warm the hearths of the thousands of homes in this Great Inland Empire!" This vision was passed on to others who finally corralled a portion of the waters to bring the dreams of the dreamers to reality. A plant was erected, cables were stretched across the desert and thrown over the mountains, and this power was put to work.

Today this storehouse of energy lights the homes of the valley, turns the wheels of industry, and pulls long trains over the mountains. It lightens the burdens and brings comfort to thousands and thousands of people along the way. As a result of someone's vision, irrigation canals bring water from the Columbia to the dry lands on the west side of the river. The trading post of White Bluffs became a town and farther on the little city of Hanford rose out of surroundings that were made lush by the flowing streams.

To the captain of the Mountain Gem these rapids were barriers—obstacles to progress. A few people came to admire them. Some were impressed by their majesty. Others were depressed because of the heat and dusty surroundings. To those who lived close by their roar was a song in the night by which they were soothed to sleep. But the young engineer saw more than all of them. He saw leaping from them a million horses whose energy he harnessed to the tasks of mankind. What a vision!

White Bluff Charley, the Nez Perce

While waiting at White Bluffs one day for the arrival of the Mountain Gem, I met up with a party of Indians who were camping along the river. Among them was a weather-beaten man, past middle age, who was nervously waiting for the arrival of the steamer. Upon opening a conversation with him I discovered that he was White Bluff Charley who had achieved considerable notoriety in the past by his exploits during the trouble between the whites and the Nez Perces. He had lived along the river for years, had a few horses on the range, but was broke most of the time. That was his trouble now. His use of English was limited as was my use of his language—the "Chinook," as they called it—which was in reality a mixture of his own and the Spanish-French of the early Hudson Bay traders and the French voyageurs.

With the use of the few words, terms, and phrases which I had picked up along the way and with much gesturing, I ascertained that he had lost what money he had while sitting at the card table the night before. Now he wanted

162

to go down the river but he was broke. I gleaned from what he said that he had been wounded in an encounter with the white people during their struggle against confinement to the reservation and that as a member of the nontreaty bands he was seeking to eke out his living as best he could. He unbuttoned his shirt and showed me an ugly scar, dangerously near his heart, where a white man's bullet had struck him. Though a child of a peaceable tribe the expression of hate and pain showed deeply on his countenance as he alluded to this incident. When he was given the money required for his fare his wrinkled face lit up with a light which reflected something beautiful in the life of this poor bruised child of nature who could not forget the undeserved treatment that he and his people received at the hands of the white folks. As he walked up the gangplank he kept looking back and repeating his phrase of gratitude—"skookum man"!

As I listened to his story and that of his kinsmen, I wondered again and again what atonement the usurpers of their liberty can ever make for their mistreatment of those whose lands they confiscated and for all the wrongs they endured at the hands of those who often, according to tradition and history, misused or mishandled the compensatory measures provided for these dispossessed people. Our record of handling Indian affairs will hardly stand the close scrutiny of the Great Judge nor of those who had hoped for better treatment.

White Bluff Charley has long since gone to his last hunting grounds. Let us hope that his lot there may be a happier one than that which he experienced in his career while he lived among us.

Buckaroo Brown

Buckaroo Brown was a child of the plains. While we lived in the desert our paths often crossed and he frequently stopped at our home. Because of that he comes into this narrative again and again. In fact, he became so well acquainted that he often turned his extra saddle horses into our pasture when he scouted the range in the section where our holdings lay. He had his eyes open for stock that belonged to us and one day he turned over to us a beautiful, unbranded two-year-old chestnut sorrel mare that he took from an outlaw band, as compensation for the kindness we had shown him.

From him I learned much of the lore of the range. He told me how to ascertain the age of horses, not by looking into their mouths and evaluating their age by their teeth, but at their tails. He said that if that appendage was curly it meant that the horse was below two years old. If it was wavy he was called a shedder, that is, he was in the years when he shed his baby teeth. After the hair of his tail became straight he was known in the language of the range as a willow tail, which meant that he had come to the age when he was developing what horsemen called a smooth mouth. During this period he lost the cups in his teeth and some of the molars were beginning to wear down to where sharp edges developed. Beyond that period his tail began to mat, that is, the loose hair collected at the lower end and formed a clump that increased until it became so large as to interfere with his speed when chased by horsemen.

From him I learned, too, the calls that quieted the wild horses when brought under control. These peculiar notes and sounds were heard all the way across the range from Texas to the Canadian line and no doubt beyond. I learned, too, that wild horses can be led but not driven. Often I saw this lone horseman at the head of a small band he had picked up, soothing them with his call and leading them with their necks arched, as though hypnotized, into the pasture or corral. When in a moment they ventured to run or make a break for freedom, he swerved his saddle horse slightly in the direction toward which they inclined and immediately they were again under his command.

He was a son of the out-of-doors. I am not able to say whether he could read or write. He certainly was not learned in the knowledge of the schools, but he knew all the ways of the open spaces. All the sounds of the out-of-doors had a meaning to him—he could predict fairly well the weather by the howl of the coyotes. In fact, he was practically as successful as the trained specialists of our day.

I shall always remember the ride for horses in the Saddle Mountains. The bands that feed in the hills are the hard ones to get. They know all the trails, many of which are mere paths where they travel single file. Some of them overhang as it were gorges hundreds of feet deep. To follow them in such surroundings takes matchless skill and sure-footed mounts that never make a wrong step. One day a band of them had ventured out of the mountain into the foothills, almost into the plains. At first sight of us they hied to the security of their favorite retreat. I always credited Brown with having at least as much sense as a horse but this time I was wrong. In planning his strategy, he had missed. Instead of separating as we later discovered we should have done and approaching them from opposite directions we took the wrong trail and came upon them following a path that literally hung on the side of a ledge with a deep abyss below. They made their escape. In following them my horse suddenly turned on a path so narrow that a person on foot probably would have done so with caution. But she was the sure-footed chestnut sorrel with white stockings that never let me down and she made the turn safely.

My last meeting with Brown came one day shortly before I left the desert for good. He rode up to the cabin one September afternoon to give me some information that I wanted him to get and for a last word. We had johnnycakes, eggs, and ham for supper. After we had finished the meal he lingered a while, then he mounted Roany and rode away. Within the next day or so I turned Babe, my only remaining saddle horse, over to my brother and drove to the railroad with a freighting outfit to make my exit from the land that once was home.

What happened to Brown? As long as Henry Gable lived I understand he remained a lone ranger in the wide Columbia Flat and beyond to Moses Lake or farther still to places where horses roamed. The last information I had of him was that one day he started northward, with a band of horses. Whither he was bound no one seemed to know. He just disappeared perhaps as mysteriously as he had come. Often when with him he spoke of the Peace River country in northwestern Canada. Perhaps that's where he is now— if he still rides the range!

Gibson the Cherokee

John Gibson was a half-breed Cherokee Indian. He claimed to have been born in what he termed lapland—the place where Oklahoma laps over Texas or vice versa, depending on the direction from which the wind blows. Early in his boyhood he began trading. His chief stock consisted of dogs and hound-dogs such as he accumulated throughout the community. In later years when he became more mature he switched from the canine family to horses and mules. He made his way to Texas and followed the ranch life with all its variations. He rode trail herd, took part in the round-up, and after the advent of barbwire he took his turn in fence riding.

Somewhere in Texas he found a girl that came from a wealthy stockman's home and married her. She was a good wife but cooking was not her specialty. In Texas where beef was plentiful she had learned to fry steak and make soda biscuits with surprising skill. Beyond that her culinary

166

abilities were limited except that she could boil eggs. Some people said that she also was a Cherokee, but in appearance she was a white woman.

John was a trader all the days of my acquaintance with him. He was one of the best friends I had but he was not above taking advantage of a person in a horse trade. Knowing this I always followed the maxim of the range land, "Let the buyer beware," and succeeded in getting along with him in all our transactions.

His home was some three or four miles removed from a frontier horse town. He had some stock on the range and several times I did some riding for him. Once when my wife had gone to visit her brother at Prosser I stayed with them. During the winter season they moved to a dilapidated section of the town known as Chickasaw Flat, a miserably noxious place of old shanties and shacks filled with half-breeds, children, unwashed and uncombed, and a veritable nest of mangy, flea-bitten dogs, lousy cats, and all kinds of animal and insect life that breeds and thrives in such surroundings.

But John and his family were above that level of existence and when spring came they moved back to the cabin on the ranch. After the performance of satisfying ablutions they settled down to a normal way of living for the summer.

Once when we were in town John disappeared and when he later showed up he carried under his arm a red salmon fish whose tail fin reached to the sidewalk. That meant that for the next day or two, or three there would be much meat at the Gibson table.

When we settled down to partake of the fish we discovered that there was but one knife available. "The kids lost the rest," is what the mistress of the Gibson Manor said. Whatever her cooking may have lacked in other respects, there was nothing derogatory to be said about her fried meats, hot bread, and coffee, according to my taste.

167

For some reason John trusted me. He, himself, could not write, he simply made his mark. I often wrote his checks, checked over his bankbook, wrote some of his promissory notes, and was entrusted with other matters that indicated the confidence I held in his heart. Once he gave me a gold mounted fountain pen as a token of his appreciation. He was ordinarily peaceable but when his temper flared, as it sometimes did, he was dangerous. Several times when he was on the point of getting into serious trouble I got him to leave town. Under such circumstances he always took my advice although he was years older than I. One day when he had been too indulgent with this thirst, he became quarrelsome and for a time things looked bad. When I said to him, "John! Let's get out of town," he holstered and followed me to the livery barn where we got our horses and hit the trail, as the saying was. After his temper was down and he was sober he thanked me for what I did for him that day. He was a typical Texan-Oklahoman-Washingtonian Cherokee with faults galore but he was always kind to my wife and me. He was our friend!

And Others Also

But there were others also from all parts of the compass who ate at our table or rode the trails we did and braved the heat and dust along the way. Time and space are not available to tell of the Bailey girls, homesteaders, whose father was a Spokane lawyer, nor of Miss Pruder and Miss Macy, schoolteachers from the same city, nor of Miss Burly, an optician who came from Kansas City. Dr. Cassel was a practicing physician who left her medical practice in Boston to share the life of the frontier with her brothers, the Winspears', who lived on the brow of the bluff overlooking the Koontz Coulee. She was the one hope of all that vast section when sickness set in and one of the very few that remained to pioneer through the years long after the rest of us left

the country. Nor can we overlook Frenchy, who had spent
years on the Pampas of Argentina, or Harry Gray, once a
football player on the Iowa University team. From the hills
of Tennessee had come the Haley boys, who stayed on after
we left and are now owners of a large cattle ranch. Then
there was Abe Harder, the hobo-printer-lawyer, and Elmer
Thompson, the fine businessman whose thirst finally
dragged him into oblivion, the Summers and the Bair boys
and Fay Ballard and Gus—good old Gus Grundi! And perhaps the most precious of all our friends were the Guthries—
George and Mary—missionaries returned from India, where
George was manager of the Methodist Publishing House
until his health broke. What memories rise out of the past
as these names come up before us!

Almost a half century has passed since that day when as
a young man I rode out of the sage into a new untrodden
way which the Master had planned for me. I see again this
host—all of them—as they were when I left them. What
an array of manhood and womanhood, of culture, professions, and occupations the desert had drawn to itself! Some
of their names are forgotten now but their faces rise before
us as they were then, untouched by the years that have since
passed by. They were our neighbors and fellow residents
with whom we shared the desert!

Will you not come home, brother,
  Home to us again?
I have a balm for bruised hearts,
  Sleep for waking eyes—
Says the warm wind, the west wind
  Full of desert cries.

From "The Westland"

XVII

The Return of the Prodigal

Years after we left the scene of our pioneering I returned to see what Father Time had done to the place that was once our home. When I came up over the rim of Sunflower Flat it seemed as though the Saddle Mountains were broadly smiling their greeting, and the sage bushes nodded to each other in a friendly way and said: "The prodigal has returned —we knew he would." I went to the little knoll where years before we stood—Emma and I and little Myron—and decided that here is where we would drive down our stakes and build the cabin that was to become our home on the range. Across the little draw is where we built shelters for the stock and eventually an enclosure which was given the dignified name of a corral. Once the place teemed with life, simple though it was. Magazines, journals, and books from the outside world kept us from rusting out and the neighbors, though widely scattered and few, with an occasional band of buckaroos, constituted the world that went past our door—a long, thin line it was!

At the time of my return everything was changed. The miles of fence that we had so laboriously built around our holdings were gone—posts, barbwire, and all. So was our cabin which had been a very simple structure. At the time of our sojourn, however, it was one of the most comfortable ones in all that country. The corral and stables were gone too, as were all the cabins from the large Koontz Coulee to the Saddle Mountains, except the Winspear spread which was turned into a wheat ranch. No one knows where all this material went, nor does it make any difference. No doubt some squatter or perhaps some horsemen who were in need of the material took it.

All that remained of what was home and its possessions was the old teakettle. It was battered and badly dented and gave evidence of hard usage and much abuse. Over the years after we left, it saw men come and go. It heard the wind shriek and the coyotes howl on many a dismal night and felt the heat of the summer suns for years. Its nose was badly askew and its wide mouth was twisted out of shape and was deformed and lacerated. But when I stooped to wipe the dust away from it, it seemed that a smile broke from the pitifully misshapen lips of this poor distorted and disfigured remnant of our possessions as it tried to greet me and say, "So you have come home!" As I stood by it a whole world of mine that is now gone seemed to fall in upon me. Then the teakettle began to talk.

"Do you remember," it said, "the morning when the man came to buy your stove after you decided to leave the country? After its merits had been discussed the mistress of the house set me on top of the high copper reservoir and

172

said, with a faint quiver in her voice, 'The teakettle goes with the stove.' The next day she was dressed in a lovely new black skirt and a white blouse when you together drove to White Bluffs for your last trip across the Columbia to do some shopping at the Trading Post. When you came home I concluded from your conversation that the stove was sold. Then I wondered anxiously what kind of person my new mistress would be. Do you remember when you told your wife how pretty she looked that day, she said, 'But what good did it do? Hardly anyone saw me.' But I saw her and you saw her, and I was proud that I belonged to her. Then she was young and slender—almost a girl. Her hair and eyes were dark and she was so brave, full of courage, and self-reliant. She always kept me burnished and polished until I glittered and gleamed. Then she set me on the reservoir where she could admire me. On the long days when she was alone, often homesick and lonely, she set me on the stove and while the water boiled and bubbled and simmered I sang for her the sweetest song I knew."

It continued, "You know when the man came for the stove after you were gone he set me aside and said, 'My wife doesn't want this old thing'; so I stayed in the house all alone. Sometimes rough-looking horsemen with dust-covered faces and goatskin chaps came and set me on the brush fire to heat water for their coffee. Sometimes sheepherders used me too. But no one polished my sides any more or seemed to care how I looked or what happened to me. When one day I scalded the hand of a careless buckaroo he said some high words and kicked me off the fire into the brush. There I lay for a long time wishing for my mistress to heal my bruises and make my face to shine once more, but she never came.

"One day some strange men came and tore down the house where we, you and I, had lived. Then they took down the corral and the sheds and hauled all the materials away.

173

Since then I have been here all alone and have known no shelter and no kindness. Only rough hands have handled me until now I am so battered and marred that I cannot even hold water and am no longer of any use to anyone. Sometimes when these unkind travelers pass through the land and stop here to prepare their meals or eat their lunch, someone will pick me up and say, 'Oh, here is a teakettle. We'll have some coffee!' Then when he sees my battered sides he gives me another kick and passes on.

"Yes, I remember your little boy, the only child within miles when you lived here. He played with his little wagon, his dog and cat, the little lariat you made for him, and Babe, your saddle horse, and your saddle. They were his only playmates except his mother. Since you left, the roundup has gone through here almost every year with thousands of horses in the herd. While the buildings were standing and the fences were still in place they sometimes held the remuda in our pasture. In the wintertime the sheepmen camped around our buildings with their thousands of sheep and lived in our house.

"Do you recall," it asked, "the time when you came home from a long ride along the mountains and had a baby coyote in a gunny sack strapped on your saddle? Neither I nor my mistress nor the old house cat were in favor of harboring that noxious animal and we were all glad when one day while you were gone he dug himself out of his cage and ran away."

At first I suspected that my wife had something to do with his release, but she stoutly denied it. Even though he belonged to the wild, it seemed that there was something about us that he liked, for he was often seen with a bit of rope around his neck, loitering near the buildings where we lived. No doubt he got his food with less trouble while he was in our custody than after he had made his escape.

"One day before you moved away," the teakettle mused,

"when I was all alone, some strange, nicely dressed good people stopped here and cooked their meal. Then I saw one of them place a new five-dollar bill between the lids of your wife's Bible. Do you recall the time," it said, "when you cooked for the men that worked for you, the winter when your wife had gone far away to her people? Over there is where their tent stood in which they had stored their belongings and where they slept. Each morning they filled their sheet iron heater with sagebrush to warm their sleeping quarters before they got up. How the smoke used to roar out of the stovepipe which often became red-hot! What an excitement there was when one windy morning the tent was set on fire and the men had no time to dress! And how their shirts fluttered in the cold wind as they dashed hither and yon trying to rescue their grips and clothing from the flames!

"Then there was your last Thanksgiving Day when you drove away to a neighbor's place over by the river for dinner. When you came home, your missus seemed much mortified and chagrined, I gleaned from the conversation, because you were amused when the host lost control of the goose he was carving and a piece of the breast landed in his lap, and your mirth increased when a drumstick got out of hand, swished across the table, and came nigh hitting you in the chest.

"The winter when your wife was gone," it said, "you came home one time with the odds and ends of hogs which you helped John Gibson, the half-breed Cherokee, butcher and worked them up into liverwurst. Do you recall what a mess that was that you and I cleaned up?"

Yes, I remembered! I had gone to Connell for supplies one day and had the spring wagon loaded and ready to start on the twenty-five-mile homeward drive early the next morning. I was up long before daylight and had everything in readiness to hitch up and start. When I went to the

175

restaurant for breakfast, who should I see but a friend and neighbor who lived some miles north of us, hanging onto a lamppost in front of the eating house. He was drunk again and was singing a very doleful and unmelodious song to the full moon that was then on its way down. After breakfast I loaded him into the spring wagon and started home. But he was an impossible passenger. When I came to the Gibson ranch some miles out of town, I stopped and unloaded. After I had him safely bedded down in a manger and covered with blankets and hay to keep him from freezing, I stayed to help Gibson with the butchering job which he had started. As the procedure progressed I learned that the heads and hocks and livers and hearts meant nothing to him. That constituted feed for the dogs and coyotes, he said. I carefully saved those choice morsels and after my passenger was sufficiently sobered I drove home and with the help of my faithful teakettle turned it all into a delicious mess of liverwurst.

"Do you remember the evening when you returned from the mountain," it recalled, "with pieces of petrified wood that so intrigued and interested you?"

Yes, I recalled. Buckaroo Brown and I had been riding along the hills for horses. Here in this barren waste there was not a sign of there ever having been a forest. Then we suddenly came upon what had evidently been a clump of trees which had by now been turned into stone. The trunks and branches lay scattered over about an acre or so. Petrified wood! This meant that at one time long ago—nobody knows when—there was sufficient moisture here to grow trees. Then the sea came in and they became covered with water, laden with silica in solution, which filtered into the pores and cells where it precipitated and replaced the woody tissue that wasted away and the trunks and branches were turned into rock. Now the sea was gone. High up on the mountainsides lay these remnants of another age while higher up still were the marks of a shore line where sea shells and sand were washed up from the deep.

This brought to mind an incident of another time when on a hot day I was riding along in the heat and dust of the barren foothills. The trail led me into a deep, narrow coulee where I found a spring that seeped out of the hillside, but which was soon lost in the sand. Along its path was a sward of green and by its side, with its roots deep in the water, stood a little tree. It was not a pretty specimen. It was knotty and gnarled, weather-beaten and deformed. All its life it had stood alone against the wind and storm. It had to fight for its existence almost every day, but it lived because it had its roots in living water. Then I realized what the psalmist had in mind when he spoke about the righteous man being like a "tree planted by the rivers of water."

"One time," the teakettle said, "when your work had taken you away from the roads to the place where there were only horse trails to follow, you told your missus approximately when she could expect you to come home. Long before that I heard you make a standing agreement with each other that if you ever failed to come at the appointed time she should set the brush pile on fire to show you the way. Now you had been delayed and she was becoming anxious."

Yes, I remembered that. Darkness had fallen and the night was becoming deep. The trail had been longer than I thought and more difficult. I had charted my way by the stars and the five points of the Rattlesnakes. The full moon was to the southeast, and the five points to the southwest. Half way between was where I thought our cabin ought to be. With these land and sky marks to guide me I tried to find the way home. Then suddenly, miles off to the south, I saw flames like a far distant lamp—then I knew where our cabin was. I knew that the hands of my wife had lit the brush pile and the burning bushes became the lodestar that guided me through the night to my own fireside.

177

But the desert also has its tragedies. One day a lonely wagon came from somewhere out of the west bearing a family and its few meager belongings. Darkness overtook them when they reached the rim of the coulee where they decided to camp till morning. That night when the wind was sighing their sick baby died. They were far from home and friends in a land where there were but few people, none of whom they knew. Then by the light of the moon the father dug a little grave by the side of the road. When the morning broke they wrapped the child in a blanket and laid it on a soft bed of hay which the father had prepared. While the mother and children stood by he covered it up and rounded the little mound with his shovel as well as he could, as a last token of his love. Then they left it alone.

I often passed the spot and as I went by it seemed like holy ground because here in the bosom of the earth lay this treasure wrapped in its mother's love. I wonder where this family is now. They were young then and their children were small, but their minds must often wander back across the miles to this lonely place. No doubt the winds and rain have long since obliterated every trace of the cradle of hay that is covered with earth. They could hardly find it now if they would, but God knows where it is. Many times when I went by I saw the butterflies fluttering over the few flowers that grew around the spot where the soil had been disturbed. I am sure if the mother had seen them she would have liked to think that they were little angels guarding her baby asleep in the desert by the side of the dusty trail.

Then my reverie was broken and the teakettle spoke again. "Do you still live in a little house? And do you sit easily in the saddle as you used to and swing the lariat for a throw? Does your missus ride gracefully as she did when she was here in the desert? Is her hair still glossy and black and are her eyes dark as they were then? And your little boy, where is he?"

"No," I replied, "I live in the city now where the streets are hot and where masses of people congregate. I no longer ride. There is no room for horses and no need to swing a lariat. I am a minister and preach the Gospel to people. I am connected with a school and spend my time in an office at a desk or in the classroom where I have taught many hundreds of young people how to live right and have tried to help them become Christians. My wife's hair is white now and the little boy you knew has grown into manhood and has two sisters."

Then the time had come to leave. I looked again at the battered form of this last remnant that tied me to the place that once was our home and wished that my wife could have been there to share this experience with me; for just one last glimpse into the past where we had lived together. I turned to go, but after the overwhelming flood of memories which this weather-beaten friend of other years had stirred up, I felt almost like a sinner to leave it there alone. It seemed like deserting a child in the embrace of this wide unoccupied waste of land. When I reached the little raise where some rods away the corrals had been, I turned for a last look at the spot which was so hallowed with many memories. Then I closed my eyes on the scene and left. As I went through the sagebrush it seemed that I heard a familiar voice calling almost pleadingly: "Does your missus have a teakettle?"

Today those years lie deeply in the past, but they are as sharply engraved on memory's walls as though they had been carved with an iron pen upon a rock. Sometimes in my dreams I ride again and feel the bite of the breezes that blow from the snow peaks or the sting of the hot sand that is swept from the plains, as the "Knights of the Saddle" go galloping by. Oftentimes the aroma of sagebrush or the smell of freshly baked soda biscuits or boiling beans or frying bacon brings up scenes of the far days that are gone.

179

And on nights when sleep eludes me and phenobarb fails, then I do not count sheep in order to coax slumber to my tired eyes. Nor do I count cattle as Marguerite Wallace Kennedy does—I count horses!

EPILOGUE

MORNIN' ON THE DESERT

Mornin' on the desert, and the wind is blowin' free,
And it's ours, jest for the breathin', so let's fill up, you and
    me.
No more stuffy cities, where you have to pay to breathe,
Where the helpless human creatures move and throng and
    strive and seethe.

Mornin' on the desert, and the air is like a wine,
And it seems like all creation has been made for me and
    mine.
No house to stop my vision, save a neighbor's miles away,
And the little dobe shanty that belongs to me and May.

Lonesome? Not a minute! Why, I've got these mountains
    here,
That were put here just to please me, with their blush an'
    frown an' cneer.
They're waitin' when the summer sun gets too sizzlin' hot,
An' we jest go campin' in 'em with a pan an' coffee pot.

Mornin' on the desert—I can smell the sagebrush smoke,
I hate to see it burnin', but the land must sure be broke.
Ain't it just a pity that wherever man may live
He tears up much that's beautiful that the good God has
      to give?

Sagebrush ain't so pretty? Well, all eyes don't see the
      same.
Have you ever saw the moonlight turn it to a silvery flame?
An' that greasewood thicket yonder—well, it smells just
      awful sweet
When the nightwind has been shakin' it—for its smell is
      hard to beat.

Lonesome? Well, I guess not. I've been lonesome in a
      town,
But I sure do love the desert with its stretches wide and
      brown.
All day through the sagebrush here the wind is blowin'
      free,
And it's ours jest for the breathin', so let's fill up, you and
      me.

*—Author unknown. Found tacked to the door of a southern
Nevada deserted desert cabin. Courtesy, "Nevada," Highways
and Parks.*